Physical Characteristics of the
Australian Shepherd

(from the American Kennel Club breed standard)

Back: Straight and strong, level and firm from withers to hip joints.

Tail: Straight, docked or naturally bobbed, not to exceed four inches in length.

Coat: Hair is of medium texture, straight to wavy, weather resistant and of medium length. The undercoat varies in quantity with variations in climate.

Hindquarters: The width of the hindquarters is equal to the width of the forequarters at the shoulders. Stifles are clearly defined, hock joints moderately bent. The hocks are short, perpendicular to the ground and parallel to each other when viewed from the rear.

Color: Blue merle, black, red merle, red—all with or without white markings and/or tan (copper) points, with no order of preference.

Size: The preferred height for males 20–23 inches, females 18–21 inches.

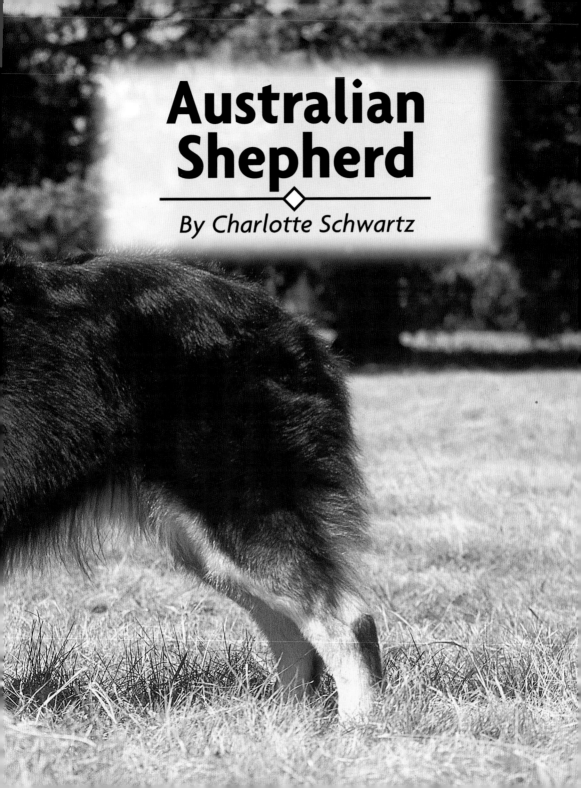

Australian
Shepherd

◆

By Charlotte Schwartz

Contents

Australian Shepherd

KENNEL CLUB BOOKS: AUSTRALIAN SHEPHERD
ISBN: 1-59378-279-9

Copyright © 2000 • Revised American Edition: Copyright © 2003
Kennel Club Books, Inc., 308 Main Street, Allenhurst, NJ 07711 USA
Cover Design Patented: US 6,435,559 B2 • Printed in South Korea

PHOTO CREDITS:

Norvia Behling, Mary Bloom, T.J. Calhoun, Carolina Biological Supply, Doskocil, Isabelle Français, James Hayden-Yoav, James R. Hayden, RBP, Carol Ann Johnson, Bill Jonas, Dwight R. Kuhn, Dr. Dennis Kunkel, Mikki Pet Products, Antonio Philippe, Photo-take, Jean Claude Revy, Alice Roche, Dr. Andrew Spielman, Karen Taylor, Alice van Kempen. Illustrations by Renée Low.

Although its name suggests a dog of Australian heritage, the Australian Shepherd was developed in the European Basque country, the USA and Mexico, as well as in Australia. Today the breed is typically known as being of American origin.

History of the
AUSTRALIAN SHEPHERD

The scene is a cattle ranch in the heart of the American Southwest. A herd of cattle is being moved from one grazing area to another. Two ranch hands on horseback keep watch over every move the huge animals make. Two small figures, Australian Shepherds, are busy on the periphery of the herd, keeping the cows together and moving toward new pastureland.

Suddenly, one of the cows decides she doesn't want to be herded and strikes out at the dogs with her back feet flying. Just as quickly, the dogs flatten themselves on the ground directly behind her as her hooves fly above the dogs but miss them completely. Within seconds, the dogs rise up and rush in to bite at the cow's heels, convincing her that moving with the herd is the most prudent thing to do. One does not try to outmaneuver an Aussie!

Like all working Australian Shepherd dogs, these two will work the cattle for hours on end, traveling mile after mile in the course of a workday. By night, they will bed down near their master and, in their silence, keep watch over home and family. Then, before daybreak, they will once again hit the trail to keep the stock safe and together.

Australian Shepherds are strong, athletic, agile and quick. They move effortlessly across the land in their work of herding livestock. Their size and intelligence make them ideal at working cattle, but they can often be found herding sheep and goats as well. Classified as working or herding dogs, their genetic makeup demands they be kept busy and allowed to employ their keen sense of duty in order to be content with life.

Perhaps the most interesting thing of all about Aussies, as they are affectionately called, is that they are not Australian dogs at all. They originated in America and have subsequently found favor among herdsmen around the world. Well, you might say, if they're not originally from Australia, why are they called Australian Shepherds?

That is an interesting question with an even more interesting answer. Let us look at their history: where and how they developed as a breed will help us understand the kind of dog they have become. Only then can we make an informed decision about

Aussies are bred to be working dogs— they are strong, athletic, agile and fast. They were developed originally as sheep herders, but once their true potential was recognized they came to be used with all types of livestock. No job was too big for Aussies!

whether or not to share our lives with an Aussie.

AN AMERICAN ORIGINAL

The Aussie's story begins back in the late 18th century and early 19th century in the Pyrenees of northern Spain and southwestern France, the area known as the Basque country. There, the hills were alive with sheep and herdsmen who were known as Basques. To help manage their flocks over the mountainous terrain, they used small dogs to herd the sheep and guard the flocks as they grazed.

In the early 1800s, herdsmen were in great demand in Australia due to the rise of the wool market. As work in the Basque region of Europe was slowing down, some of the Basque herdsmen took their dogs and went to Australia, where they could find work.

Eventually, the Australian sheep were shipped to America, where the wool market was also growing. It was inevitable that some of these Basque herdsmen and their dogs would follow the sheep to America.

In the New World, men and dogs found the terrain and weather conditions in the southwestern United States similar to what they had known in Europe. Thus, they adapted easily, some of them even migrating as far south as Mexico. In years to come, those dogs would be known as New

> **GENUS *CANIS***
> Dogs and wolves are members of the genus *Canis*. Wolves are known scientifically as *Canis lupus* while dogs are known as *Canis domesticus*. Dogs and wolves are known to interbreed. The term *canine* derives from the Latin-derived word *Canis*. The term "dog" has no scientific basis but has been used for thousands of years. The origin of the word "dog" has never been authoritatively ascertained.

Mexican Shepherds. They were simply a larger version of the smaller Basque dogs. The increased size of the dogs meant that they could be used to herd cattle as well as sheep.

Then, in the mid-to-late 1800s, the famous Gold Rush occurred in the West. The wool market soared even higher and, as more and more sheep were raised to meet the demand, more dogs were needed for herding. The small Basque-like dogs were bred with the larger Mexican dogs and some other herding breeds with strong genetic traits for the work of herding and guarding. As they had originally come from

The attention-grabbing merle coloration, for which the breed is noted, is a pattern of dark blotches over a light-colored background. In the blue merle, shown here, black against white or light gray gives the illusion of a blue tone.

Australia, people began calling them Australian Shepherds. Eventually, they became known as Aussies.

SPECIAL FEATURES

The distinctive merle coloration was probably one of the first features to draw people's attention to the breed. Merle is a color pattern of dark blotches over a lighter-colored background. For example, a blue merle consists of black blotches against a white or very light gray background that creates an illusion of the color blue.

Once the breed became noticed, people discovered its calm nature and intelligence. Cattlemen soon became inter-

ested in the breed and, before long, cattle ranches in America's West were maintained by Australian Shepherds. These dogs proved to be the perfect size to work a herd of cattle in pairs. A single dog might find a herd of kicking, butting and goring cattle a bit too much to handle, but two dogs had no trouble managing the herd.

Soon, Aussies were used to herd all kinds of livestock: turkeys, geese, ducks, cattle, sheep, goats, reindeer, buffalo and even bison, the toughest of all stock animals. Now the breed had truly achieved its potential as a great American herder, and the name Australian Shepherd became official.

This appreciation for the breed continued into the early 1900s when the West was populated with ranches and large farms. It seemed the wool market kept growing. As the demand for more and better wool kept rising, so, too, did the demand for more livestock dogs. The Australian Shepherd was the nation's answer to the demand.

The dogs fulfilled the stockmen's need for a large, strong and assertive breed to work cattle and, at the same time, were a calm breed to work sheep. Though there were other herding breeds available, some of those other breeds were too quick and too excitable, making control more difficult. However, the Aussie, with his imperturbable nature and deliberate work pattern, perfectly fit the bill! Thus, the Aussie established itself firmly throughout Colorado, California, Arizona, Oregon and wherever large properties were used for raising livestock in the western United States.

THE SECRET IS OUT—BREED CLUBS ESTABLISHED

Great secrets, however, are rarely kept for long. Soon the virtues of the Aussie became known to people in other parts of the country. Once the secret of this wonderful dog became common knowledge among dog lovers in the midwestern and eastern United States, Australian Shepherds began appearing across the country. Suburban families welcomed these highly intelligent and trainable dogs into their homes.

By the mid-1950s it was apparent that a national breed club was needed to ensure the true genetic background of the Australian Shepherd breed. Thus, in 1957, the Australian Shepherd Club of America was founded in Tucson, Arizona. This club is still the parent club of the Australian Shepherd. The official registry for the breed was the International English Shepherd Registry, also known as the National Stock Dog Registry. The United States

Australian Shepherd Association also monitors the breed. With rules for perpetuating the breed clearly spelled out by a governing breed club, breeders would have a set of written guidelines to follow. Size, type and color as well as physical structure were defined. The issues of character, temperament and working ability were also addressed. In other words, little was left to chance for continuing the unique qualities of the breed.

BRAIN AND BRAWN

Since dogs have been inbred for centuries, their physical and mental characteristics are constantly being changed to suit man's desires for hunting, retrieving, scenting, guarding and warming their masters' laps. During the past 150 years, dogs have been judged according to physical characteristics as well as functional abilities. Few breeds can boast a genuine balance between physique, working ability and temperament.

A NEW KIND OF AUSSIE

It was in the 1950s that an interesting phenomenon occurred. Similar to what had happened to some of the world's hunting breeds a century before, Australian Shepherds needed to develop a type of personality to fit their new role as companion dogs, better suited to a suburban lifestyle.

In the case of the hunting dogs, their tireless energy was just too much for the suburban dweller. Thus, dogs with calmer temperaments were bred to each other to produce dogs that could cope with life in a less active suburban home. The two types of hunting dogs then became known as field dogs (for actual hunting) and bench dogs (for companions and exhibiting in the breed ring at dog shows).

That same great stamina that helped carry Aussies effortlessly across the land in their job of herding, plus their single-minded devotion to one master, were traits not needed in the modern lifestyle. They would have to develop a new type of personality better suited to families in the suburbs. Their work drive would have to soften so that they could live and be happy in a less active setting.

In suburbia, owners usually go to work and leave their dogs home alone during the day, so

The Aussie developed a new type of personality as it evolved from a herding breed into a wonderful companion animal. Aussies were selectively bred together to produce dogs better suited to suburban, rather than farm, life.

Conformation Aussies are generally larger, flashier and more heavily coated than their working counterparts. They are quite a striking presence in the show ring.

Aussies would have to make an adjustment. Furthermore, in his new role as companion, the Aussie would need to broaden his devotion to include entire families. He would also need to be friendly toward family friends and guests as well as children.

To better understand this new role for Aussies, I consulted a well-known breeder by the name of Caterina O'Sullivan of Howell, New Jersey.

"We still have working Aussies out West," Ms. O'Sullivan assured me, "but we have also developed what we call a conformation dog. This Aussie can be shown in the breed ring as well as serve a vital role of companion to individuals who are not ranchers yet who admire Australian Shepherd qualities."

"What exactly is the difference between the two types of Aussies?" I asked.

"Working Aussies are called stock dogs. They are lighter-boned, quick and dedicated to their master and working the herds. Conformation Aussies are bigger-boned, heavier-coated flashier dogs. They have lots of eye appeal and make beautiful presentations in the show ring with their lush coats and lovely colors."

The irresistible Aussie charm, good looks, even temperament, hardiness and love of humans have made it so popular that the breed became one of the top 50 in the American Kennel Club's registry. One look at this adorable Aussie pup and it's not hard to see how the breed won so many admirers!

"What about temperament?"

"That, too, has changed to accommodate their new role. The conformation dogs are friendly, devoted to their families and, when raised with children, are dedicated protectors of the little ones in their charge. Though Aussies can be aloof toward strangers, they readily accept those to whom their owners show friendship."

True to his reputation of devotion, intelligence and adaptability, the Australian Shepherd, it seems, does not disappoint in his newest role as companion dog. Out on the range, the Aussie is a strong, agile herder that can work any kind of livestock. In suburbia, the Aussie offers companionship of the highest order with his loyalty, his intelligence and his athletic ability.

Whether stock dog or companion, the beauty of the Australian Shepherd makes him one of the top 50 registered breeds with the American Kennel Club. He is also registered with the United Kennel Club. In America, Australian Shepherds are shown in the Herding Group and in England they are classified as an Interim Breed in the Pastoral Group. Other countries currently experiencing an increased interest in the breed are Canada, Germany, France, Spain, Japan and Belgium.

It was an English physician, Dr. Johannes Caius, who in 1570 wrote a treatise on the marvels of

working shepherds. In it, he spoke of the dog's wagging its tail in response to its master's voice and waving fist. He told how the shepherd dog moved and guarded the flocks and recovered the wandering weathered (neutered) rams back to the fold.

Finally, the doctor reported how the shepherd benefited from the dog's efforts while he himself expended minimal physical effort. Little did the doctor realize it, but he could have written those very same words about Australian Shepherds in the 21st century!

Today we realize that as far as herding dogs are concerned, nothing has changed over the centuries. The dogs have always been and will continue to be better than any machine invented for guarding and moving groups of animals.

Once properly socialized, the Aussie quickly adapts to life in the home with children, cats and most other pet and farm animals.

Characteristics of the
AUSTRALIAN SHEPHERD

The very first time we set eyes on an Australian Shepherd, we are struck by the symmetry and balance of the dog. Neither a little dog nor a large one, the Aussie stands somewhere between 18 and 23 inches at the withers (highest point of shoulder). He is slightly longer than he is tall and possesses good bone structure. His coat, which is unique in color to each individual dog, is of moderate length and coarseness. The coat beneath his throat and around his neck is called the ruff. The long hair beneath his front legs and under his chest is called feathering (more often seen in males than females).

The Australian Shepherd is a moderate dog in all respects. His appearance bespeaks agility,

The Australian Shepherd is a very beautiful dog. It is well balanced and symmetrical, and stands a little under 2 feet tall at the shoulder.

strength and stamina. His heavy coat and bobtail give the impression that he's well equipped for life in the outdoors. His build tells of his physical abilities, and his demeanor and facial expression indicate his intelligence and determination to get the job done.

There is no doubt in the minds of all who meet him that he is capable of performing his work while devotedly serving his owner as friend and partner. He is an enthusiastic worker, a devoted companion and an excellent guardian of home and family. Males carry a distinctive look of masculinity about them, while females are usually a bit smaller and more feminine in overall appearance. In other words, it's easy to distinguish the difference between the sexes by sight.

OWNER CONSIDERATIONS

With regard to behavior, Aussies are not normally dog-aggressive nor are they fence-climbers or diggers. Unlike some of the hunting breeds, they do not have a genetic predisposition to run away from home and master. Indeed, as they strive to please their owners, they prefer to stay close to home.

They do not like being separated from their families, so crate training is a wise choice. Then, when they must be left alone, they can stay in their crates where they feel secure.

In addition, they aren't chewers, so they can be offered a variety of toys such as soft, fluffy ones, flying discs and hard chew bones, which will help keep their teeth clean.

All dogs, however, need to be supervised when playing with toys to make sure they don't swallow or choke on pieces of toys that get broken off. When a toy begins to get tattered and gnawed out of shape, discard it and give the dog a new one.

If you allow your dog to run free in a fenced yard, the fence should be at least four feet high. Even though Aussies aren't fence-jumpers, the four-foot height would discourage any thoughts of scaling it to go wandering through the neighborhood.

THE IDEAL OWNER

There are two types of ideal Australian Shepherd owners. Let's

The facial expression of the Australian Shepherd tells the story of an intelligent dog who is more than eager to please and share affection with his owner.

Although a wonderful pet for many, the Aussie is a working dog at heart and, thus, must have his attention diverted with plenty of safe toys and activity.

banite. Though the owner's professional life may demand that he work indoors, he is the kind of person who uses his free time and days off to get outdoors and do things with his dog. He is a person who needs to keep physically fit and active, an athletic individual who makes a point of spending some time each day outside. Furthermore, he is not discouraged by reasonable extremes in temperature or moderate amounts of rain.

Conversely, the person who enjoys spending his free time in quiet activities such as reading and watching television would not make an ideal Aussie owner. Australian Shepherds are not "couch potatoes" and do not do well, either physically or emotionally, in passive lifestyles.

An Aussie can cope with living indoors in a small apartment or house, providing the owner joins him during part of each day in some form of vigorous outdoor activity. Given this lifestyle, the Aussie quickly learns that his master's arrival home means great sport will soon be enjoyed. Given a stretch of bad weather or an owner who is recovering from an illness, the Aussie can be exercised indoors by teaching him a trick or in some way stimulating his mental abilities.

Another consideration for the ideal Aussie owner is the enjoyment of brushing his dog regu-

look at both of them. Then you can decide if, in fact, you fit into either category.

The farmer or rancher is the most desirable Aussie owner. In an environment where the dog must work every day, he is capable of making herding and guarding decisions while working long hours, even in rough weather. Aussies like nothing better than to help their owners with whatever chores need doing.

The second type of ideal Aussie owner is the active subur-

Never far from his working background, the intelligent and tractable Aussie can be taught to aid his owner in a variety of tasks. He's a willing and able helper!

larly, as in several times a week or whenever the dog's coat collects foreign matter such as grass clippings, seeds or leaves.

AUSSIE PERSONALITY

INTUITIVENESS
As an Aussie owner, I have found them to be extremely sensitive to my emotions. For example, if I am happy and/or excited, the dogs are too. However, when I'm sad or tired or just not feeling well, they are subdued and silent while staying close to me in quiet concern. Nervousness, such as that experienced in preparing for a dog show or going on a trip, usually results in the dogs' experiencing anxiety as well. In other words, Aussies, it seems, are intuitive animals who are aware of and sensitive to their owners' moods and to situations going on around them, and they react accordingly.

DOGS, DOGS, GOOD FOR YOUR HEART!
People usually purchase dogs for companionship, but studies show that dogs can help to improve their owners' health and level of activity, as well as lower a human's risk of coronary heart disease. Without even realizing it, when a person puts time into exercising, grooming and feeding a dog, he also puts more time into his own personal health care. Dog owners establish more routine schedules for their dogs to follow, which can have positive effects on their own health. Dogs also teach us patience, offer unconditional love and provide the joy of having a furry friend to pet!

SOCIABILITY
Possibly the most interesting attribute of Aussies is the manner in which they relate to strangers. They are, by nature, reserved toward those whom they don't

Even Aussies need to relax! Quiet time with his owner is just as important to the pet Aussie as regular activity.

know. They are not openly aggressive toward strangers, as is common with many of the working breeds. Rather, they choose to ignore those they don't know, providing that they (the strangers) do not threaten their masters or families.

Devoted to their owners, Aussies constantly keep track of their charges while ignoring others in their environment. Take an Aussie out among people and he will, in all probability, focus his attention on his owner while acting as if there is no one else present.

However, if the owner chooses to speak to or interact with another person, he merely has to introduce his dog to the stranger and the Aussie will accept the person's attention. Aussies are polite, reserved and non-aggressive dogs who openly demonstrate their loyalty to their owners while exhibiting restrained good manners to others.

AFFECTION

Along with loyalty, the Aussie demonstrates great affection for his owners. He loves a scratch behind the ears or a hearty pat on the side. If allowed, he'll nuzzle next to his owner and will often use those expressive eyes to beg for attention in return.

INTELLIGENCE

Perhaps the most valuable attribute of the Aussie is his intelligence. If we define intelligence as being genetically engineered to perform tasks for and/or with humans, then the Aussie is among the most intelligent of breeds. He can work side-by-side with his master at such chores as carrying things, fetching objects and even pulling small carts containing farm supplies. He can also herd

---

DO YOU WANT TO LIVE LONGER?

If you like to volunteer, it is wonderful if you can take your dog to a nursing home once a week for several hours. The elder community loves to have a dog with which to visit, and often your dog will bring a bit of companionship to someone who is lonely or somewhat detached from the world. You will be not only bringing happiness to someone else but also keeping your dog busy—and we haven't even mentioned the fact that it has been discovered that volunteering helps to increase your own longevity!

cattle at great distances from his master, who may be a quarter of a mile away. Often an Aussie will be sent to search for an errant sheep who has wandered away from the flock. He will have to search for the animal and, once located, he will have to find the quickest and safest route back to the flock.

Speaking of decision-making, my own black and white Aussie named Fancy was a living example of a dog's working away from her owner's side and making decisions without assistance. She was a tracking dog. Her story exemplifies the versatility of the Australian Shepherd.

She was originally owned by her breeder. Kept as a brood bitch, she produced two litters of puppies, both of which produced several breed champions. However, following her second litter, Fancy developed a medical problem and she had to be spayed, thus ending her puppy-bearing career.

I met Fancy when she was three years old and her owner was looking for a home for her where she would be loved and possibly worked in obedience to keep her busy. At the time, I was looking for a new tracking dog and decided that Fancy and I could give it a try as a team. Fancy needed something to do and a family to love while I needed a new tracking partner. I knew that I would love her.

At our first meeting, Fancy was polite but paid me very little attention. Gail, her owner, suggested I put her on a collar and leash and take her for a walk away from their property. At first, Fancy kept looking back toward home as we headed down the road, but I ignored the behavior and kept talking to her. As we got further away from her home, Fancy began to look up at me as if to say, "Where are you taking me?"

GUARDIAN INSTINCTS

There are some confirmed reports about some Aussies that have taken action to pull children in danger out of harm's way. In each case, the dogs acted alone and without the direction of humans. Their genetic traits of guarding and protecting have been so strong that they made their own decisions to save their young charges. They are independent thinkers in their work and beyond!

TAKING CARE

Science is showing that as people take care of their pets, the pets are taking care of their owners. A recent study published in the *American Journal of Cardiology* found that having a pet can prolong his owner's life. Pet owners generally have lower blood pressure, and pets help their owners to relax and keep more physically fit. It was also found that pets help to keep the elderly connected to their communities.

I just kept up a soft-voiced conversation and reassured her that all was well. Finally, we came to a field where I found a large stick in the grass alongside the road. I picked it up and tossed it a few feet away.

As I did, I showed it to Fancy and said something like, "See this? Want this? Fetch it, girl!"

To my astonishment, Fancy ran forward and grabbed the stick immediately. "Wow," I thought to myself, "this is a natural-born retrieving Aussie. I bet she'll make a great tracker."

By the time we reached Fancy's home and breeder again, we were friends and Fancy kept asking with those big dark brown eyes to throw the stick "just once more." I knew then that we'd make a match and I think Fancy knew it, too.

The story of Fancy ends many years later when she died of old age. She had become an excellent tracking dog and was able to find people who had been missing for several days and were miles away. How she did it, no one will ever know. She used her nose to follow the person's scent trail and her bright mind to decide what was and what was not pertinent information in the environment where she was working.

One of the most valuable lessons I ever learned came from Fancy and some of my other tracking dogs, which was to never doubt what your dog knows. He cannot tell you what he knows or how he knows it. Just trust that because of his phenomenal scenting and hearing abilities, he will always know more than you do. I have honored that lesson for over thirty years and it has never failed me. Unfortunately, because dogs can't speak our language, we must learn to trust them and believe what they tell us by their behavior. That's a difficult lesson for most humans.

VERSATILITY

The Australian Shepherd is a most versatile breed. Though happiest when working with sheep or cattle on the ranch, the Aussies that don't live on ranches find fulfillment by adapting to the lifestyles of their owners in other settings such as suburbia.

A house with a pool makes an exciting environment for swimming. Aussies will learn to love the water if they're introduced to it at a very young age and will eagerly join their owners for a cool dip in summertime.

Aussies love to travel, too. They make great travelers for folks who take driving vacations. Trained to be calm and quiet, they make excellent motel guests and people often don't even know there's a dog nearby because the Aussie doesn't bark or whine needlessly.

Campers, hikers, boaters and owners who enjoy spending time in the great outdoors find that bringing their Aussies with them makes the activities even more fun. Since Aussies are constantly keeping watch over their owners, they don't wander away from the campsite in search of other dogs or animals. They are content to stay close to their masters,

Aussies need exercise and activity, and they make great playmates. Retrieving games are fun for both owner and dog.

whether hiking through the forest or sitting around a campfire.

Finally, I'd be remiss if I didn't mention the sport of agility and how Aussies react to it. Let me assure you that it is a sport for which Aussies seem to have a natural affinity—they excel at it and they love it!

REQUIREMENTS OF OWNING AN AUSSIE

Dogs that do in life what they were originally bred to do are dogs that are happy, well-adjusted individuals. Short of performing tasks for which they were intended, the dogs can be happy

BOBBED TAILS

Some Aussies are born with naturally bobbed tails. Others are born with tails that must then be docked. When docking, the tail must be cut so that no more than four inches is left. By the time the Aussie is fully grown, the short bob is barely distinguishable at a glance.

The Aussie's abundant coat needs regular attention to stay healthy and looking its best. Aussies should be trained to accept brushing when they are still puppies.

and content if their owners make an effort to substitute activities that closely resemble the original purpose of the breed.

Herding dogs can be taught to "herd" a large rubber ball around the house, keep an eye on the children or family cat and make decisions regarding where and when their toys should be put away at the end of the day. Being physical means being active, whether indoors or out. If an owner can find ways to substitute natural behaviors for ones more suited to his chosen lifestyle, then his Aussie can be a vital part of the family unit.

Aussies also need some grooming to keep their coats shining, clean and free from parasites. They need regular dental care, toenail clipping and ear cleaning, too. Most of these requirements can be done at home without the expense of a professional groomer.

They need good-quality food and fresh water at all times. They should be bathed several times a year to keep them looking their best. However, most of all, they need love and attention from their owners. They are not solitary animals.

VIRTUES AND DRAWBACKS

It should be abundantly clear that Australian Shepherds make exceptionally fine companions for the person who wishes to get involved with his dog. The Aussie is a hands-on, "let's-work-together" breed of dog and the more an Aussie becomes involved in his owner's lifestyle, the happier the dog will be.

The drawbacks of the breed are few, but significant. They do need routine grooming in the form of brushing. Brushed on a regular schedule to remove dead hair and foreign matter, they will always look their best and feel good.

Even more important is the Aussie's need for activity. An owner who lives a sedentary life is not suitable as an Aussie owner. It's unfair to the dog to provide

him with insufficient or meaningless activities. Furthermore, it can be miserable for the owner who suddenly discovers that his Aussie has developed some very undesirable behaviors caused by frustration and lack of exercise.

What type of dog can keep up with the seemingly boundless energy of a young person? The Aussie, of course!

BREED-SPECIFIC HEALTH CONCERNS

Generally speaking, the Australian Shepherd is a healthy breed of dog. Aussies do not suffer from the wide variety of diseases and genetic problems and anomalies experienced by many other breeds. However, it is possible for them to become subject to certain health problems, some of which are hereditary.

CORRECTIVE SURGERY

Surgery is often used to correct genetic bone diseases in dogs. Usually the problems present themselves early in the dog's life and must be treated before bone growth stops.

To determine the probability of a puppy's getting any of these hereditary health problems, the prospective buyer should question the breeder about the health history of the parents. If the breeder refuses to discuss the matter, look for another litter of puppies and another breeder. Buying a puppy from a person who either denies health problems or refuses to discuss them is just asking for trouble in the months to come.

EYE PROBLEMS

Juvenile cataracts have been found in some Australian Shepherds and are hereditary. Appearing as a cloudiness over the lens of the eye, cataracts will eventually cause blindness in the dog.

A veterinary ophthalmologist can determine whether or not a puppy is carrying the genes for juvenile cataracts. Reputable breeders usually take entire litters to the ophthalmologist for testing prior to selling any of the puppies.

The Canine Eye Registration Foundation (CERF) is a monitoring registry that reports on eye problems in pure-bred dogs. CERF can provide certification of normal-eyed dogs. Responsible breeders have their breeding stock certified and will give the puppy buyers documentation from CERF, showing the eye health of the parents and the puppies.

Puppies as young as eight weeks of age can be examined for cataracts. Cataract-removal surgery is a consideration and most often very successful. A full consultation with the ophthalmologist is recommended.

Left: The typical posterior subcapsular cataract appears between one and two years of age in dogs. It rarely progresses to where the dog has visual problems. Right: Inherited cataracts generally appear between three and six years of age, and progress to the stage shown here where functional vision is significantly impaired.

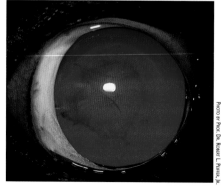

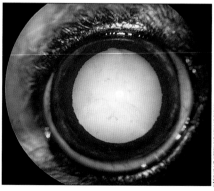

PHOTO BY PROF. DR. ROBERT L. PEIFFER, JR.

PHOTO BY PROF. DR. ROBERT L. PEIFFER, JR.

DO YOU KNOW ABOUT HIP DYSPLASIA?

Hip dysplasia is a fairly common condition found in pure-bred dogs. When a dog has hip dysplasia, its hind leg has an incorrectly formed hip joint. By constant use of the hip joint, it becomes more and more loose, wears abnormally and may become arthritic.

Hip dysplasia can only be confirmed with an x-ray, but certain symptoms may indicate a problem. Your dog may have a hip dysplasia problem if it walks in a peculiar manner, hops instead of smoothly runs, uses its hind legs in unison (to keep the pressure off the weak joint), has trouble getting up from a prone position or always sits with both legs together on one side of its body.

As the dog matures, it may adapt well to life with a bad hip, but in a few years the arthritis develops and many dogs with hip dysplasia become crippled.

Hip dysplasia is considered an inherited disease and only can be diagnosed definitively when the dog is two years old. Some experts claim that a special diet might help your puppy outgrow the bad hip, but the usual treatments are surgical. The removal of the pectineus muscle, the removal of the round part of the femur, reconstructing the pelvis and replacing the hip with an artificial one are all surgical interventions that are expensive, but they are usually very successful. Follow the advice of your veterinarian.

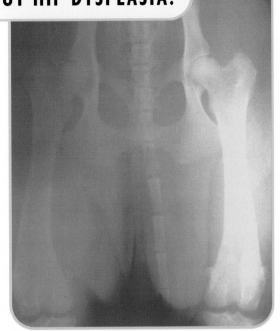

(Above)
X-ray of a dog with "Good" hips.

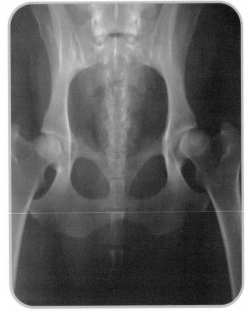

(Left)
X-ray of a dog with "Moderate" dysplastic hips.

CANCER

Cancer has been known to occur in some Aussies. It cannot be considered a common problem, but owners need to be aware of the possibility. Treatment is sometimes effective but, as in humans, it can also result in an early demise.

HIP DYSPLASIA (HD)

Hip dysplasia is genetically transmitted in Aussies and is a developmental problem of the hip joint. Dogs born with a "susceptibility factor" for HD should be monitored carefully to prevent their becoming overweight or over-exercised at a very young age while the bones are still developing. Basic conformation of the individual dog and caloric intake are also contributory factors in producing dysplastic dogs.

By age 24 months, dogs can be x-rayed to determine whether or not they have HD. If the answer is affirmative, a realistic program of maintenance can be instituted to minimize the dog's suffering and manifestation of motor problems.

Under some circumstances, surgery is called for and is usually successful in relieving pain, though the dog may be left with a permanent limp.

Based on x-ray diagnosis, the Orthopedic Foundation for Animals (OFA) rates the quality of the hip joint as excellent, good, fair, borderline or dysplastic. From this analysis, responsible breeders choose dogs for their breeding programs who are certified free of hip dysplasia.

HYPOTHYROIDISM

Hypothyroidism is a hormonal problem. Though it is difficult to diagnose and has several potential causes, it is usually easy to treat with medication. Some of the types of thyroiditis can begin early in life. However, they often don't become clinically apparent until later in life after the dog reaches three years of age.

OTHER PROBLEMS

A small number of Aussies have developed other health problems such as collie eye, some cardiac conditions, epilepsy, elbow dysplasia and allergies. Since these problems have appeared in very few Australian Shepherds, they cannot be considered breed problems.

SKIN PROBLEMS

Eczema and dermatitis are skin problems that occur in many breeds and they can often be tricky problems to solve. Frequent bathing of the dog will remove skin oils and will cause the problem to worsen. Allergies to food or something in the environment can also cause the problem. Consider asking the vet about homeopathic remedies in addition to conventional treatment.

Hardiness is part of the Australian Shepherd's nature and, as such, he generally makes a very healthy pet if properly cared for, fed, exercised and checked by the veterinarian.

AUSTRALIAN SHEPHERD

Whenever we refer to the standard of a breed, we are actually talking about the standard of perfection of that breed. The standard of perfection of a breed is a word picture that describes in detail exactly what the ideal specimen should look like. In addition, most standards include some reference to temperament and character, so the overall picture of the breed is made clear.

Judges use the standard in determining the best dog presented to them on any given day in conformation classes. Breeders use the standard of the breed to produce puppies that will grow into adult dogs closely resembling the ideal specimen, both in physical appearance and temperament.

The American Kennel Club (AKC) is guided in its description of the Aussie by the Australian Shepherd Club of America, the parent club that upholds and enforces the standard in the US. Following is an excerpt from the AKC standard.

AKC STANDARD FOR THE AUSTRALIAN SHEPHERD

General Appearance: The Australian Shepherd is an intelligent working dog of strong herding and guarding instincts. He is a loyal companion and has the stamina to work all day. He is well balanced, slightly longer than tall, of medium size and bone, with coloring that offers variety and individuality. He is attentive and animated, lithe and agile, solid and muscular without cloddiness. He has a coat of moderate

---

BREEDER'S BLUEPRINT

If you are considering breeding your bitch, it is very important that you are familiar with the breed standard. Reputable breeders breed with the intention of producing dogs that are as close as possible to the standard and that contribute to the advancement of the breed. Study the standard for both physical appearance and temperament, and make certain your bitch and your chosen stud dog measure up.

In conformation showing, the judge feels under the coat to check for correct body construction and bone structure.

length and coarseness. He has a docked or natural bobbed tail.

Size, Proportion, Substance:
Size—The preferred height for males is 20–23 inches, females 18–21 inches. Quality is not to be sacrificed in favor of size. Proportion—Measuring from the breastbone to rear of thigh and from top of the withers to the ground the Australian Shepherd is slightly longer than tall. Substance—Solidly built with moderate bone.

Head: Clean cut, strong and dry. Overall size should be in proportion to the body. The muzzle is equal in length or slightly shorter than the back skull. The muzzle tapers little from base to nose and is rounded at the tip.

Expression: Showing attentiveness and intelligence, alert and eager. Gaze should be keen but friendly. Eyes are brown, blue, amber or any variation or combination thereof, including flecks and marbling. Almond shaped, not protruding nor sunken. The blue merles and blacks have black pigmentation on eye rims. The red merles and reds have liver (brown) pigmentation on eye rims. Ears are triangular, of moderate size and leather, set high on the head. At full attention they break

"Intelligent, attentive and alert" are words used to describe the Aussie's expression—this dog's face embodies them all beautifully.

protuberance. Length and width are equal. Moderate well-defined stop.

Nose: Blue merles and blacks have black pigmentation on the nose (and lips). Red merles and reds have liver (brown) pigmentation on the nose (and lips). On the merles it is permissible to have small pink spots; however, they should not exceed 25% of the nose on dogs over one year of age, which is a serious fault.

Teeth: A full complement of strong white teeth should meet in a scissors bite or may meet in a level bite.

Neck, Topline, Body: Neck is strong, of moderate length, slightly arched at the crest, fitting well into the shoulders. Topline—Back is straight and strong, level and firm from withers to hip

forward and over, or to the side as a rose ear. Prick ears and hanging ears are severe faults.

Skull: Top flat to slightly domed. It may show a slight occipital

Short back without desired tuck-up.

Correct strong, level topline, with moderate tuck-up.

Incorrect upright ears.

Correct triangular ears of moderate size.

MEETING THE IDEAL

The AKC defines a standard as: "A description of the ideal dog of each recognized breed, to serve as an ideal against which dogs are judged at shows." This "blueprint" is drawn up by the breed's recognized parent club, approved by a majority of its membership and then submitted to the AKC for approval.

The AKC states that "An understanding of any breed must begin with its standard. This applies to all dogs, not just those intended for showing." The picture that the standard draws of the dog's type, gait, temperament and structure is the guiding image used by breeders as they plan their programs.

joints. The croup is moderately sloped. Chest is not broad but is deep with the lowest point reaching the elbow. The ribs are well sprung and long, neither barrel chested nor slab-sided. The underline shows a moderate tuck-up. Tail is straight, docked or naturally bobbed, not to exceed four inches in length.

Forequarters: Shoulders—Shoulder blades are long, flat, fairly close set at the withers and well laid back. Legs straight and strong. Bone is strong, oval rather than round. Pastern is medium length and very slightly sloped. Dewclaws may be removed. Feet are oval, compact with close knit, well arched toes. Pads are thick and resilient.

Hindquarters: The width of the hindquarters is equal to the width of the forequarters at the shoulders. Stifles are clearly defined, hock joints moderately bent. The hocks are short, perpendicular to the ground and parallel to each other when viewed from the rear.

Coat: Hair is of medium texture, straight to wavy, weather resistant and of medium length. The undercoat varies in quantity with variations in climate. Hair is short and smooth on the head, ears, front of forelegs and below the hocks. Backs of forelegs and britches are moderately feathered. There is a

The typical effortless-looking movement of the Australian Shepherd. Notice the convergence of forelegs and hindlegs when the Aussie is running at top speed.

moderate mane and frill, more pronounced in dogs than in bitches.

Color: Blue merle, black, red merle, red—all with or without white markings and/or tan (copper) points, with no order of preference. White is acceptable on the neck (either in part or as a full collar), chest, legs, muzzle underparts, blaze on head and white extension from underpart up to four inches. White on the head should not predominate, and the eyes must be fully surrounded by color and pigment. Merles characteristically become darker with increasing age.

Gait: A smooth, free and easy gait. He exhibits great agility of movement with a well-balanced, ground covering stride. Fore and hind legs move straight and parallel with the center line of the body. As speed increases, the feet (front and rear) converge toward the center line of gravity of the dog while the back remains firm and level. The Australian Shepherd must be agile and able to change direction or alter gait instantly.

Temperament: An intelligent, active dog with an even disposition; he is good natured, seldom quarrelsome. He may be somewhat reserved in initial meetings.

AUSTRALIAN SHEPHERD

PUPPY APPEARANCE
Your pup's appearance tells much about his overall health and soundness. Your puppy should look well-fed but not have a distended abdomen, which may indicate worms or incorrect feeding, or both. The body should be firm, with a solid feel. The skin of the abdomen should be pale pink and clean, without signs of scratching or rash. The breeder should have removed dewclaws from the hindquarters, and possible the forequarters, as mentioned in the breed standard.

Part of your research into Australian Shepherds should consist of practical information, which you can use in choosing and living with your new puppy. Any special characteristics of either males or females are worth investigating. In the case of Aussies, there is little, if any, difference in personality between the sexes. Females tend to be rather more gentle, males more assertive. Both, however, are extremely intelligent, active, attentive and loving.

Aussies mature between 18 and 22 months of age and have an average lifespan of 11 to 15 years. Litters average between five and eight puppies. If you don't plan to show, they make ideal companions when the females are spayed and males are neutered.

Once you've completed the preliminary investigation of the breed, perhaps even gone to a dog show or two, it's time to visit some breeders. You'll meet the parents of the puppies and observe the litter as well.

First, the breeder should be willing and eager to discuss the general health of the parents of the litter. Ask questions about specific health problems such as hip dysplasia and eye health. Ask if the parents and puppies have tested free of genetic health problems. Does the breeder have Orthopedic Foundation for Animals (OFA) and Canine Eye Registration Foundation (CERF) certification to substantiate the results of those tests?

If you encounter a breeder who is unwilling to discuss the health of the puppies and adult dogs, find yourself another breeder. This is not a person with whom you should be doing business because a reputable breeder is very concerned about the health of his dogs and their genetic contribution to future generations.

Next, ask to see a pedigree of the puppies. A pedigree is the history of the dog's family tree. It lists the registered names of parents, grandparents and great-grandparents on both the puppy's mother's and father's sides. It also gives information about degrees and titles that those relatives have earned. That information can provide you with a better understanding of the physical conformation and behavioral accomplishments of the puppy's family. From that, you can draw more realistic goals for the puppy you will eventually choose.

ARE YOU PREPARED?

Unfortunately, when a puppy is bought by someone who does not take into consideration the time and attention that dog ownership requires, it is the puppy who suffers when he is either abandoned or placed in a shelter by a frustrated owner. So all of the "homework" you do in preparation for your pup's arrival will benefit you both. The more informed you are, the more you will know what to expect and the better equipped you will be to handle the ups and downs of raising a puppy. Hopefully, everyone in the household is willing to do his part in raising and caring for the pup. The anticipation of owning a dog often brings a lot of promises from excited family members: "I will walk him every day," "I will feed him," "I will house-train him," etc., but these things take time and effort, and promises can easily be forgotten once the novelty of the new pet has worn off.

PET INSURANCE

Just like you can insure your car, your house and your own health, you likewise can insure your dog's health. Investigate a pet insurance policy by talking to your vet. Depending on the age of your dog, the breed and the kind of coverage you desire, your policy can be very afford-able. Most policies cover accidental injuries, poisoning and thousands of medical problems and illnesses. Some carriers also offer routine care and immunization coverage, which are more costly than the others, but may be well worth the investment.

HOMEWORK

Do your homework when decid-ing to buy a puppy. Read about all the breeds that interest you.

Find the one that best fits your lifestyle. Go to dog shows and observe the breed in the show ring. Talk to breeders and show-dog handlers. Listen carefully to what they say about the best qualities and even the problems of the breed of your choice.

Finally, find a breeder who has a litter of puppies for sale. Call in to see them. When you do, have the following list of considerations in mind as you visit the puppies and their parents.

1. When you arrive, look around the place before you look at the litter. Is it clean? Does it smell clean? Is there a place for the puppies to play, eat and sleep, or are they crowded into a small

By observing the puppy with one of its parents, you can get a fair idea of the pup's eventual size, looks and temperament.

space on newspaper that is covered with food droppings and feces?

2. When you first see the litter, do they come running to you in friendly anticipation or do they run away and cringe in fear?

3. What about the parents? Are they well cared for and clean? Are they friendly, standoffish, aggressive? You should know that the temperament of the parents is probably what the puppies will inherit when they grow up. Puppies, in particular, should be friendly and happy with little or no sense of protectiveness when young.

4. No doubt you will have an opportunity to observe some puppy feces. Is the stool well formed and solid? Loose, runny stool is a cause for concern and should be investigated by a veterinarian who will be looking for the cause of the problems, such as worms, infection, bacterial infestation, etc.

5. How do the puppies interact with the breeder? They should not show fear but instead be happy to see him and anxious for attention. If you observe one particular puppy sitting off in a corner by himself, that puppy is not a good candidate for you. It will probably grow up to be shy, perhaps even a fear-biter.

6. As your eyes (and your heart!) gravitate toward one particular puppy, take a good look at it. Is

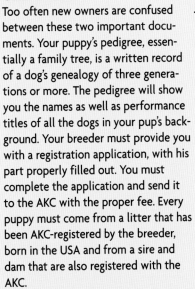

PEDIGREE VS. REGISTRATION CERTIFICATE

Too often new owners are confused between these two important documents. Your puppy's pedigree, essentially a family tree, is a written record of a dog's genealogy of three generations or more. The pedigree will show you the names as well as performance titles of all the dogs in your pup's background. Your breeder must provide you with a registration application, with his part properly filled out. You must complete the application and send it to the AKC with the proper fee. Every puppy must come from a litter that has been AKC-registered by the breeder, born in the USA and from a sire and dam that are also registered with the AKC.

The seller must provide you with complete records to identify the puppy. The AKC requires that the seller provide the buyer with the following: breed; sex, color and markings; date of birth; litter number (when available); names and registration numbers of the parents; breeder's name; and date sold or delivered.

it clean? Does it smell good with sweet puppy breath? Are its eyes bright and shiny, its nose cool and not running? Is it free of a cough? Is it also free of parasites such as fleas?

7. Check out the sex of the puppies that interest you. Before you begin your shopping expedi-

tion, you should have decided which sex is better for you and your family. Keep in mind that pet dogs should either be spayed (females) or neutered (males) before they reach maturity.

8. Does the breeder have all of the required paperwork? Proper registration papers will go with the puppy and show you as the owner. A feeding schedule and whatever else you will need to make the puppy's transition from birth home to your home as easy and stress-free as possible are necessary.

A pedigree showing at least three generations should accompany the puppy. Last, but not least, a veterinary certificate showing the puppy's immunization record is essential. From this record, your own veterinar-

It's easy to succumb to the charms of an adorable Aussie ball of fluff, but use your head, not just your heart, in selecting your pup.

PUPPY SELECTION

Your selection of a good puppy can be determined by your needs. A show potential or a good pet? It is your choice. Every puppy, however, should be of good temperament. Although show-quality puppies are bred and raised with emphasis on physical conformation, responsible breeders strive for equally good temperament. Do not buy from a breeder who concentrates solely on physical beauty at the expense of personality.

ian will proceed with future immunizations and health maintenance.

At last, you've chosen a new puppy and now you face a whole new future filled with the wonder of owning a canine companion.

COMMITMENT OF OWNERSHIP

Before you select your puppy, you should have already made some very important decisions. Your breed of choice is the Australian Shepherd, which means that you have decided which characteristics you want in a dog and what type of dog will best fit into your family and lifestyle. If you have selected a breeder, you have gone a step further—you have done your research and found a responsible, conscientious person who breeds quality Australian Shepherds and who should become a reliable source of help as you and your puppy adjust to life together. If you have observed a litter in action, you have obtained a firsthand look at the dynamics of a puppy "pack" and, thus, you should have learned about each pup's individual personality—perhaps you have even found one that particularly appeals to you.

However, even if you have not yet found the Australian Shepherd puppy of your dreams, observing pups will help you learn to recognize certain behavior and to determine what a pup's behavior indicates about his temperament. You will be able to pick out which pups are the leaders, which ones are less outgoing, which ones are confident, which

RELEASE ME

Breeders rarely release puppies until they are eight to ten weeks of age. This is an acceptable age for most breeds of dog, excepting toy breeds, which are not released until around 12 weeks, given their petite sizes. If a breeder has a puppy that is 12 weeks or more, it is likely well socialized and house-trained. Be sure that it is otherwise healthy before deciding to take it home.

ones are shy, playful, friendly, aggressive, etc. Equally as important, you will learn to recognize what a healthy pup should look and act like. All of these things will help you in your search, and when you find

YOUR SCHEDULE . . .

If you lead an erratic, unpredictable life, with daily or weekly changes in your work requirements, consider the problems of owning a dog. The new puppy has to be fed regularly, socialized (loved, petted, handled, introduced to other people) and, most importantly, allowed to go outdoors for house-training. As the dog gets older, it can be more tolerant of deviations in its feeding and relief schedule.

the Aussie that was meant for you, you will know it!

Researching your breed, selecting a responsible breeder and observing as many pups as possible are all important steps on the way to dog ownership. It may seem like a lot of effort... and you have not even taken the pup home yet! Remember, though, you cannot be too careful when it comes to deciding on the type of dog you want and finding out about your prospective pup's background. Buying a puppy is not—or should not be—just another whimsical purchase. This is one instance in which you actually do get to choose your own family! You may be thinking that buying a puppy should be fun—it should not be so serious and so much work. Keep in mind that your puppy is not a cuddly stuffed toy or decorative lawn ornament, but a creature that will become a real member of your family. You will come to realize that, while buying a puppy is a pleasurable and exciting endeavor, it is not something to be taken lightly. Relax...the fun will start when the pup comes home!

Always keep in mind that a puppy is nothing more than a baby in a furry disguise...a baby who is virtually helpless in a human world and who trusts his owner for fulfillment of his basic needs for survival. In addition to food, water and shelter, your pup needs care, protection, guidance and love. If you are not prepared to commit to this, then you are not prepared to own a dog.

"Wait a minute," you say. "How hard could this be? All of

my neighbors own dogs and they seem to be doing just fine. Why should I have to worry about all of this?" Well, you should not worry about it; in fact, you will probably find that once your Australian Shepherd pup gets used to his new home, he will fall into his place in the family quite naturally. But it never hurts to emphasize the commitment of dog ownership. With some time and patience, it is really not too difficult to raise a curious and exuberant Australian Shepherd pup to be a well-adjusted and well-mannered adult dog—a dog that could be your most loyal friend.

PREPARING PUPPY'S PLACE IN YOUR HOME

Researching your breed and finding a breeder are only two aspects of the "homework" you will have to do before taking

"YOU BETTER SHOP AROUND!"

Finding a reputable breeder that sells healthy pups is very important, but make sure that the breeder you choose is not only someone you respect but also someone with whom you feel comfortable. Your breeder will be a resource long after you buy your puppy, and you must be able to call with reasonable questions without being made to feel like a pest! If you don't connect on a personal level, investigate some other breeders before making a final decision.

Above all, your Aussie pup must be healthy and sound.

your Australian Shepherd puppy home. You will also have to prepare your home and family for the new addition. Much as you would prepare a nursery for a newborn baby, you will need to designate a place in your home that will be the puppy's own. How you prepare your home will depend on how much freedom the dog will be allowed. Whatever you decide, you must ensure that he has a place that he can "call his own."

When you bring your new puppy into your home, you are bringing him into what will become his home as well. Obviously, you did not buy a puppy so

QUALITY FOOD

In addition to the many expenses related to the care of your Australian Shepherd, the cost of food must be mentioned. All dogs need a good-quality food with an adequate supply of protein to develop their bones and muscles properly. Most dogs are not picky eaters but, unless fed properly, can quickly succumb to skin problems.

that he could take control of your house, but in order for a puppy to grow into a stable, well-adjusted dog, he has to feel comfortable in his surroundings. Remember, he is leaving the warmth and security of his mother and littermates, as well as the familiarity of the only place he has ever known, so it is important to make his transition as easy as possible. By preparing a place in your home for the puppy, you are making him feel as welcome as possible in a strange new place. It should not take him long to get used to it, but the sudden shock of being transplanted is somewhat traumatic for a young pup. Imagine how a small child would feel in the same situation—that is how your puppy must be feeling. It is up to you to reassure him and to let him know, "Little one, you are going to like it here!"

WHAT YOU SHOULD BUY

Deciding how you will care for your Australian Shepherd before you bring him home is an important matter. Having the necessary equipment and supplies in place before you introduce the puppy or dog to his new home allows you time to give him plenty of attention rather than concentrating on purchasing dog supplies.

CRATE

Crate training should be your first consideration. Teaching the

Your young Aussie will love an open area in which to run and play, but constant supervision and secure fencing are absolutely necessary for your puppy's safety.

puppy (or grown dog) to enjoy using his crate offers protection from all types of injury to the dog, to say nothing of keeping your home safe from destructive chewing. Having his own crate provides security for the dog and gives him a safe place to stay while you are out of the home and unable to supervise him.

A common complaint from pet owners is that the dog literally destroys the house whenever he's left alone. This is called isolation frustration and occurs when the dog is given too much freedom without human supervision. The solution to the problem is offering a safe place to the dog so he has no need to be anxious about being alone. This little "cubby" or den is the answer.

ARE YOU A FIT OWNER?

If the breeder from whom you are buying a puppy asks you a lot of personal questions, do not be insulted. Such a breeder wants to be sure that you will be a fit provider for his puppy. Most breeders feel like they are adopting out one of their kids!

PHOTO COURTESY OF DOSKOCIL

do not advocate crate training, more and more breeders and trainers are recommending crates as preferred tools for show puppies as well as pet puppies. Crates are not cruel—crates have many humane and highly effective uses in dog care and training.

A crate can keep your dog safe during travel and, perhaps most importantly, a crate provides your dog with a place of his own in your home. It serves as a "doggie bedroom" of sorts—your Australian Shepherd can curl up in his crate when he wants to sleep or when he just needs a break. Many dogs sleep in their crates overnight. With soft bedding and his favorite toy, a crate becomes a cozy pseudo-den for your dog. Like his ancestors, he too will seek out the comfort and retreat of a den—you just happen to be providing him with something a little more luxurious than what his early ancestors enjoyed.

As far as purchasing a crate, the type that you buy is up to you. It will most likely be one of the two most popular types: wire or fiberglass. There are advantages and disadvantages to each type.

Your local pet shop should have a variety of crates from which you can choose one for your Aussie. Be sure to get a sturdy crate that is large enough to accommodate a full-grown Aussie.

The crate size should be big enough to allow the adult dog to lie down with its legs outstretched and to stand up without its head touching the top. To someone unfamiliar with the use of crates in dog training, it may seem like punishment to shut a dog in a crate, but this is not the case at all. Although all breeders

A TASTY BRIBE

Use treats to bribe your dog into a desired behavior. Try small pieces of hard cheese or freeze-dried liver. Never offer chocolate as it has toxic qualities for dogs.

CRATE-TRAINING TIPS

During crate training, you should partition off the section of the crate in which the pup stays. If he is given too big an area, this will hinder your training efforts. Crate training is based on the fact that a dog does not like to soil his sleeping quarters, so it is ineffective to keep a pup in a crate that is so big that he can eliminate in one end and get far enough away from it to sleep. Also, you want to make the crate den-like for the pup. Blankets and a favorite toy will make the crate cozy for the small pup; as he grows, you may want to evict some of his "roommates" to make more room. It will take some coaxing at first, but be patient. Given some time to get used to it, your pup will adapt to his new home-within-a-home quite nicely.

For example, a wire crate is more open, allowing the air to flow through and affording the dog a view of what is going on around him, while a fiberglass crate is sturdier. Both can double as travel crates, providing protection for the dog.

The size of the crate is another thing to consider. Puppies do not stay puppies forever—in fact, sometimes it seems as if they grow right before your eyes. A Yorkie-sized crate may be fine for a very young Australian Shepherd pup, but it will not do him much good for long! Unless you have the money and the inclination to buy a new crate every time your pup has a growth spurt, it is better to get one that will accommodate your dog both as a pup and at full size. A full-grown Aussie can stand up to 23 inches high at the shoulders; use this size as a guideline when purchasing the crate.

GATES

While on the subject of housing for your new dog, let's talk about baby gates. These low dividers are primarily manufactured for use in keeping children confined to certain areas. However, they are equally effective in confining dogs

Some breeders may acclimate their pups to crates before the pups leave for new homes. Once crate training begins, though, it's one pup per crate!

Wire crates are popular for use in the home.

to certain places. When you are housebreaking a puppy, you will be more successful if he is limited to small areas where you can keep an eye on him until he's completely reliable with his house-training (usually about six months of age).

BEDDING

A soft crate pad in the dog's crate will help the dog feel more at home and you may also like to pop in a small blanket. This will take the place of the leaves, twigs, etc., that the pup would use in the wild to make a den; the pup can make his own "burrow" in the crate. Although your pup is far removed from his den-making ancestors, the denning instinct is still a part of his genetic makeup. Second, until you take your pup home, he has been sleeping amid the warmth of his mother and littermates, and while a blanket is not the same as a warm, breathing body, it still provides heat and

Exercise pens are useful for keeping your Aussie secure. They are portable, so they can be easily transported for use when traveling.

something with which to snuggle. You will want to wash your pup's bedding frequently in case he has an accident in his crate, and replace or remove any blanket that becomes ragged and starts to fall apart.

TOYS

Every dog deserves to have his own toys. Toys are important tools in puppy development and should be chosen with care. Soft fabric toys or vinyl or rubber toys are good choices for young puppies, and hard bones are preferred by adult dogs. In addition, you need to supervise your puppy when he's playing with his toys. Puppies like to chew because they are teething, so they often destroy and eat toys. This is dangerous and can be avoided by supervision.

Playing fetching games with your pup and his toys is an excellent way to help him develop coordination and get some exercise, as well as quality time spent together. This is also a good way to encourage proper chewing habits and to enforce your role as pack leader. When playing with the pup and his toys, he should never use his teeth to nip at you, nor should he be aggressive or possessive regarding his toys. During playtime, if he becomes distracted and begins to chew on something else, it gives you the opportunity to give him the chew toy and praise him for chewing that instead. All of these small lessons reinforce that you are the leader, while shaping the pup's natural energies into acceptable behaviors. Remember that Aussies, in particular, are eager to develop strong bonds with their masters.

LEASH

A nylon leash is probably the best option as it is the most resistant to puppy teeth should your pup take a liking to chewing on his leash.

TOYS, TOYS, TOYS!

With a big variety of dog toys available, and so many that look like they would be a lot of fun for a dog, be careful in your selection. It is amazing what a set of puppy teeth can do to an innocent-looking toy, so, obviously, safety is a major consideration. Aussie puppies love soft, furry toys, though supervision is always sensible in case they destroy their toys. Be sure to choose the most durable products that you can find. Hard nylon bones and toys are favorites for adults, and many of them are offered in different scents and flavors that will be sure to capture your dog's attention. It is always fun to play a game of catch with your dog, and there are balls and flying discs that are specially made to withstand dog teeth.

Along with the crate, you should have a few chew toys and perhaps a soft dog bed ready to greet your new Aussie puppy.

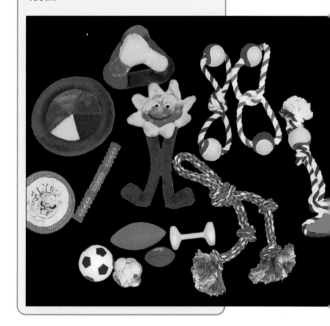

Of course, this is a habit that should be nipped in the bud, but if your pup likes to chew on his leash, he has a very slim chance of being able to chew through the strong nylon. Nylon leashes are also lightweight, which is good for a young Australian Shepherd who is just getting used to the idea of walking on a leash. For everyday walking and safety purposes, the nylon leash is a good choice. As your pup grows up and gets used to walking on the leash, you may want to purchase a flexible leash. These leashes allow you to extend the length to give the dog a broader area to explore or to shorten the length to keep the dog near you.

COLLAR

Your pup should get used to wearing a collar all the time since you

MENTAL AND DENTAL

Toys not only help your puppy get the physical and mental stimulation he needs but also provide a great way to keep his teeth clean. For adult Aussies, hard rubber or nylon toys, especially those constructed with grooves, are excellent to scrape away plaque, preventing bad breath and gum infection. For puppies, soft toys soothe their aching gums. Since stuffed toys are easily destroyed, always supervise your pup when he's playing with his soft toy.

You can purchase a suitable leash and collar for your Aussie pup from the local pet shop.

A light yet sturdy lead and collar will suffice for a young puppy. The leash will keep your curious pup securely with you as you go out and about to explore.

From the array of food and water bowls available, purchase durable, easily cleaned bowls for your Aussie.

PHOTO COURTESY OF MIKKI PET PRODUCTS.

will want to attach his ID tags to it. Plus, you have to attach the leash to something! A lightweight nylon collar is a good choice; make sure that it fits snugly enough so that the pup cannot wriggle out of it, but is loose enough so that it will not be uncomfortably tight around the pup's neck. You should be able to fit a finger between the pup and the collar. It may take some time for your pup to get used to wearing the collar, but soon he will not even notice that it is there. Snap-around collars are handy and easy to use. Buckle collars are also suitable. Chain collars are not suitable for puppies but may be needed for large strong dogs that pull when out walking.

FOOD AND WATER BOWLS

You'll also need a suitable food bowl and a separate bowl for water. These should be washed every day to avoid bacteria build-up. Once the dog has eaten his meal, the empty bowl should be removed and washed immediately. Never leave the food bowl on the floor to attract ants and other insects.

You may want two sets of bowls, one for inside and one for outside, depending on where the dog will be fed and where he will be spending time. Stainless steel or sturdy plastic bowls are popular choices. Plastic bowls are more chewable. Dogs tend not to chew

CHOOSE AN APPROPRIATE COLLAR

The **BUCKLE COLLAR** is the standard collar used for everyday purpose. Be sure that you adjust the buckle on growing puppies. Check it every day. It can become too tight overnight! These collars can be made of leather or nylon. Attach your dog's identification tags to this collar.

The **CHOKE COLLAR** can be used for training, if used properly. It is constructed of highly polished steel so that it slides easily through the stainless steel loop. The idea is that the dog controls the pressure around his neck and he will stop pulling if the collar becomes uncomfortable. Never use a chain choke collar on an Aussie pup and always remove it from the dog after training sessions.

The **HALTER** is for a trained dog that has to be restrained to prevent running away, chasing a cat and the like. Considered the most humane of all devices, it is frequently used on smaller dogs on which collars are not comfortable.

Baby gates, which are traditionally used for partitioning off rooms in the home to make them inaccessible to small children, are equally as effective for use with dogs.

on the steel variety, which can be sterilized. It is important to buy sturdy bowls since anything is in danger of being chewed by puppy teeth and you do not want your dog to be constantly chewing apart his bowl (for his safety and for your wallet!).

CLEANING SUPPLIES

Until a pup is house-trained, you will be doing a lot of cleaning. Accidents will occur, which is acceptable in the beginning because the puppy does not know any better. All you can do is be prepared to clean up any accidents. Old rags, towels, newspapers and a safe disinfectant are good to have on hand.

BEYOND THE BASICS

The items previously discussed are the bare necessities. You will find out what else you need as you go along—grooming supplies, flea/tick protection, etc. These things will vary depending on your situation, but it is important that you have everything you need to feed and make your Australian Shepherd comfortable in his first few days at home.

PUPPY-PROOFING YOUR HOME

Aside from making sure that your Australian Shepherd will be comfortable in your home, you also have to make sure that your

Devices for cleaning up after your dog will be a most welcome addition to your cache of dog supplies.

home is safe for your Australian Shepherd. This means taking precautions that your pup will not get into anything he should not get into and that there is nothing within his reach that may harm him should he sniff it, chew it, inspect it, etc. This probably seems obvious since, while you are primarily concerned with your pup's safety, at the same time you do not want your belongings to be ruined. Breakables should be placed out of reach if your dog is to have full run of the house. If he is to be limited to certain places within the house, keep any potentially dangerous items in the "off-limits" areas. An electrical cord can pose a danger should the puppy decide to taste it—and who is going to convince a pup that it would not make a great chew toy? Cords should be fastened tightly against the wall. If your dog is

PLAY'S THE THING

Teaching the puppy to play with his toys in running and fetching games is an ideal way to help the puppy develop muscle, learn motor skills and bond with you, his owner and master. Aussies are gifted and active dogs that learn coordination and muscle skills quite easily. A puppy also needs to learn how to inhibit his bite reflex and never to use his teeth on people, forbidden objects and other animals in play. Whenever you play with your Aussie, you make the rules. This becomes an important message to your dog in teaching him that you are the pack leader and control everything he does in life. Once your dog accepts you as his leader, your relationship with him will be cemented for life.

going to spend time in a crate, make sure that there is nothing near his crate that he can reach if he sticks his curious little nose or paws through the openings. Just as you would with a child, keep all household cleaners and chemicals where the pup cannot reach them.

It is also important to make sure that the outside of your home is safe. Of course your puppy should never be unsupervised, but a pup let loose in the yard will want to run and explore, and he should be granted that freedom. Do not let a fence give you a false sense of security. Although Aussies are not known for being escape artists, a fence that is not of adequate height would hardly be an obstacle for an agile Australian Shepherd. The remedy is to make the fence well embedded into the ground and high enough so that it really is impossible for your dog to get over it (at least 4 feet should suffice). Be sure to repair or secure any gaps in the fence. Check the fence periodically to ensure that it is in good shape and make repairs as needed; a very curious pup may return to the same spot to "work on it" until he is able to get through.

FIRST TRIP TO THE VET

You have selected your puppy, and your home and family are ready. Now all you have to do is collect your Australian Shepherd from the breeder and the fun begins, right? Well...not so fast. Something else you need to prepare is your pup's first trip to the veterinarian. Perhaps the breeder can recommend someone in the area who specializes in herding or working dogs, or maybe you know some other Aussie owners who can suggest a good vet. Either way, you should have an appointment arranged for your pup before you pick him up.

The pup's first visit will consist of an examination to make sure that the pup does not have any problems that are not apparent. The veterinarian will also set up a vaccination schedule; the breeder will inform you of what the pup has already received and the vet can continue from there.

INTRODUCTION TO THE FAMILY

Everyone in the house will be excited about the puppy's

coming home and will want to pet him and play with him, but it is best to make the introduction low-key so as not to overwhelm the puppy. He is apprehensive already. It is the first time he has been separated from his mother and the breeder, and the ride to your home is likely to be the first time he has been in a car. The last thing you want to do is smother him, as this will only frighten him further. This is not to say that human contact is not extremely necessary at this stage, because this is the time when a connection between the pup and his human family is formed. Gentle petting and soothing words should help console him, as well as just putting him down and letting him explore on his own (under your watchful eye, of course).

Your Aussie will revel in a soft roll in the grass, but keep in mind that parasites and allergens often are found in the lawn.

> ### PUPPY-PROOFING
> Thoroughly puppy-proof your house before bringing your puppy home. Never use roach or rodent poisons in any area accessible to the puppy. Avoid the use of toilet cleaners. Most dogs are born with "toilet-bowl sonar" and will take a drink if the lid is left open. Also keep the garbage secured and out of reach.

The pup may approach the family members or may busy himself with exploring for a while. Gradually, each person should spend some time with the pup, one at a time, crouching down to get as close to the pup's

TOXIC PLANTS

Many plants can be toxic to dogs. If you see your dog carrying a piece of vegetation in his mouth, approach him in a quiet, disinterested manner, avoid eye contact, pet him and gradually remove the plant from his mouth. Alternatively, offer him a treat and maybe he'll drop the plant on his own accord. Be sure no toxic plants are growing in your own garden.

level as possible and letting him sniff their hands and petting him gently. He definitely needs human attention and he needs to be touched—this is how to form an immediate bond. Just remember that the pup is experiencing a lot of things for the first time, at the same time. There are new people, new noises, new smells and new things to investigate, so be gentle, be affectionate and be as comforting as you can be.

PUP'S FIRST NIGHT HOME

You have traveled home with your new charge safely in his crate. He's been to the vet for a thorough check-up; he's been weighed, his papers examined; perhaps he's even been vaccinated and wormed as well. He's met the family, licked the whole family, including the excited children and the less-than-happy cat. He's explored his area, his new bed, the yard and anywhere else he's been permitted. He's eaten his first meal at home and relieved himself in the proper place. He's heard lots of new sounds, smelled new friends and seen more of the outside world than ever before.

That was just the first day! He's worn out and is ready for bed...or so you think!

It's puppy's first night and you are ready to say "Good night"—keep in mind that this is puppy's first night ever to be sleeping alone. His dam and littermates are no longer at paw's length and he's a bit scared, cold and lonely. Be reassuring to your new family member. This is not the time to spoil him and give in to his inevitable whining.

Puppies whine. They whine to let others know where they are and hopefully to get company out of it. Place your pup in his new bed or crate in his room and close the door. Mercifully, he may fall asleep without a peep. When the inevitable occurs, ignore the whining: he is fine. Be strong and keep his interest in mind. Do not allow yourself to feel guilty and visit the pup. He will fall asleep eventually.

Many breeders recommend placing a piece of bedding from his former home in his new bed so that he recognizes the scent of his littermates. Others still advise placing a hot water bottle in his bed for warmth. This latter may be a good idea provided the pup doesn't attempt to suckle—he'll get good and wet and may not fall asleep so fast.

Puppy's first night can be somewhat stressful for the pup and his new family. Remember that you are setting the tone of nighttime at your house. Unless you want to play with your pup every night at 10 p.m., midnight and 2 a.m., don't initiate the habit. Your family will thank you, and so will your pup!

THE RIDE HOME

Taking your dog from the breeder to your home in a car can be a very uncomfortable experience for both of you. The puppy will have been taken from his warm, friendly, safe environment and brought into a strange new environment—an environment that moves! Be prepared for loose bowels, urination, crying, whining and even fear biting. With proper love and encouragement when you arrive home, the stress of the trip should quickly disappear.

PREVENTING PUPPY PROBLEMS

SOCIALIZATION

Now that you have done all of the preparatory work and have helped your pup get accustomed to his new home and family, it is about time for you to have some

CHEMICAL TOXINS

Scour your garage for potential puppy dangers. Remove weed killers, pesticides and antifreeze materials. Antifreeze is highly toxic and just a few drops can kill a puppy or an adult dog. The sweet taste attracts the animal, who will quickly consume it from the floor or pavement.

fun! Socializing your Australian Shepherd pup gives you the opportunity to show off your new friend, and your pup gets to reap the benefits of being an adorable furry creature that people will want to pet and, in general, think is absolutely precious!

Besides getting to know his new family, your puppy should be exposed to other people, animals and situations, but of course he must not come into close contact with dogs you don't know well until his course of injections is fully complete. Socialization will help him become well adjusted as he grows up and less prone to being timid or fearful of the new things he will encounter. Your pup's socialization began with the breeder, but now it is your responsibility to continue it. The socialization he receives up until the age of 12 weeks is the most critical, as this is the time when he forms his impressions of the outside world. Be especially careful during the eight-to-ten-week-

old period, also known as the fear period. The interaction he receives during this time should be gentle and reassuring. Lack of socialization can manifest itself in fear and aggression as the dog grows up. He needs lots of human contact, affection, handling and exposure to other animals.

Once your pup has received his necessary vaccinations, feel free to take him out and about (on his leash, of course). Walk him around the neighborhood, take him on your daily errands, let people pet him, let him meet other dogs and pets, etc. Puppies do not have to try to make friends; there will be no shortage of people who will want to introduce themselves. Just make sure that you carefully supervise each meeting. If the neighborhood children want to say hello, for example, that is great—children and pups most often make great companions. However, sometimes an excited child can unintentionally handle a pup too roughly, or an overzealous pup can playfully nip a little too hard. You want to make socialization experiences positive ones. What a pup learns during this very formative stage will affect his attitude toward future encounters. You want your dog to be comfortable around everyone. A pup that has a bad experience with a child may grow up to be a dog that is shy around or aggressive toward children.

CONSISTENCY IN TRAINING
Dogs, being pack animals, naturally need a leader, or else they try to establish dominance in their packs. When you welcome a dog into your family, the choice of who becomes the leader and who becomes the "pack" is entirely up to you! Your pup's intuitive quest for dominance, coupled with the fact that it is nearly impossible to look at an adorable Australian Shepherd pup with his "puppy-dog" eyes and not cave in, give the pup almost an unfair advantage in getting the upper hand! A pup will definitely test the waters to see what he can and cannot do. Do not give in to those pleading eyes—stand your ground when it comes to setting rules for the pup and make sure that all family members do the

SOCIALIZATION
Thorough socialization includes not only meeting new people but also being introduced to new experiences such as riding in the car, having his coat brushed, hearing the television, walking in a crowd—the list is endless. The more your pup experiences, and the more positive the experiences are, the less of a shock and the less frightening it will be for your pup to encounter new things.

same. It will only confuse the pup when Mother tells him to get off the sofa when he is used to sitting up there with Father to watch the nightly news. Avoid discrepancies by having all members of the household decide on the rules before the pup even comes home...and be consistent in enforcing them! Early training shapes the dog's personality, so you cannot be unclear in what you expect.

(Top) This Aussie pup enjoys playing with his stuffed hedgehog toy, while (bottom) this Aussie shares his home with a real hedgehog friend.

Australian Shepherds were bred to work with other dogs and with all types of livestock; thus, they are usually comfortable around other animals.

When properly socialized, Aussies welcome affection and the friendship of humans throughout their lives.

COMMON PUPPY PROBLEMS

The best way to prevent puppy problems is to be proactive in stopping an undesirable behavior as soon as it starts. The old saying "You can't teach an old dog new tricks" does not necessarily hold true, but it *is* true that it is much easier to discourage bad behavior in a young developing pup than to wait until the pup's bad behavior becomes the adult dog's bad habit. There are some problems that are especially prevalent in puppies as they develop.

NIPPING

As puppies start to teethe, they feel the need to sink their teeth into anything available... unfortunately, that includes your fingers, arms, hair and toes. You may find this behavior cute for the first five seconds...until you feel just how sharp those puppy teeth are. This is something you want to discourage immediately and consistently with a firm "No!" (or whatever number of firm "Nos" it takes for him to understand that you mean business). Then replace your finger with an appropriate chew toy. While this behavior is merely annoying when the dog is young, it can become dangerous as your Australian Shepherd's adult teeth grow in and his jaws develop, and he continues to think it is okay to gnaw on human appendages. Born to nip at the heels of the herd, your Aussie does not mean any harm with a friendly nip, but he also does not know his own strength.

CRYING/WHINING

Your pup will often cry, whine, whimper, howl or make some type of commotion when he is left alone. This is basically his way of calling out for attention to make sure that you know he is there and that you have not forgotten about him. He feels insecure when he is left alone, when you are out of the house and he is in his crate or when you are in another part of the house and he cannot see you. The noise he is making is an expression of the anxiety he feels at being alone, so he needs to be taught that being alone is okay. You are not actually training the dog to stop making noise, you are training him to feel comfortable when he is

alone and thus removing the need for him to make the noise. This is where the crate with cozy bedding and a toy comes in handy. You want to know that he is safe when you are not there to supervise, and you know that he will be safe in his

MANNERS MATTER

During the socialization process, a puppy should meet people, experience different environments and definitely be exposed to other canines. Through playing and interacting with other dogs, your puppy will learn lessons, ranging from controlling the pressure of his jaws by biting his littermates to the inner-workings of the canine pack that he will apply to his human relationships for the rest of his life. That is why removing a puppy from its litter too early (before eight weeks) can be detrimental to the pup's development.

PUPPY PROBLEMS

The majority of problems that are commonly seen in young pups will disappear as your dog gets older. However, how you deal with problems when he is young will determine how he reacts to discipline as an adult dog. It is important to establish who is boss (hopefully it will be you!) right away when you are first bonding with your dog. This bond will set the tone for the rest of your life together.

crate rather than roaming freely about the house. In order for the pup to stay in his crate without making a fuss, he needs to be comfortable in his crate. On that note, it is extremely important that the crate is never used as a form of punishment, or the pup will have a negative association with the crate.

Accustom the pup to the crate in short, gradually increasing time intervals in which you put him in the crate, maybe with a treat, and stay in the room with him. If he cries or makes a fuss, do not go to him, but stay in his sight. Gradually he will realize that staying in his crate is all right without your help, and it will not be so traumatic for him when you are not around. You may want to leave the radio on softly when you leave the house; the sound of human voices may be comforting to him.

Sticks can be dangerous to chew, as they break easily into harmful splinters. This will not deter a determined chewer, so make sure that your Aussie, pup or adult, always has plenty of appropriate chew devices.

CHEWING TIPS

Chewing goes hand in hand with nipping in the sense that a teething puppy is always looking for a way to soothe his aching gums. In this case, instead of chewing on you, he may have taken a liking to your favorite shoe or something else that he should not be chewing. Again, realize that this is a normal canine behavior that does not need to be discouraged, only redirected. Your pup just needs to be taught what is acceptable to chew on and what is off-limits. Consistently tell him NO when you catch him chewing on something forbidden and give him a chew toy.

Conversely, praise him when you catch him chewing on something appropriate. In this way, you are discouraging the inappropriate behavior and reinforcing the desired behavior. The puppy chewing should stop after his adult teeth have come in, but an adult dog continues to chew for various reasons—perhaps because he is bored, needs to relieve tension or just likes to chew. That is why it is important to redirect his chewing when he is still young.

Your Aussie puppy relies on you for constant attention. You must be realistic when it comes to caring for your new charge.

First Aid at a Glance

Burns
Place the affected area under cool water; use ice if only a small area is burnt.

Bee stings/Insect bites
Apply ice to relieve swelling; antihistamine dosed properly.

Animal bites
Clean any bleeding area; apply pressure until bleeding subsides; go to the vet.

Spider bites
Use cold compress and a pressurized pack to inhibit venom's spreading.

Antifreeze poisoning
Induce vomiting with hydrogen peroxide. Seek *immediate* veterinary help!

Fish hooks
Removal best handled by vet; hook must be cut in order to remove.

Snake bites
Pack ice around bite; contact vet quickly; identify snake for proper antivenin.

Car accident
Move dog from roadway with blanket; seek veterinary aid.

Shock
Calm the dog; keep him warm; seek immediate veterinary help.

Nosebleed
Apply cold compress to the nose; apply pressure to any visible abrasion.

Bleeding
Apply pressure above the area; treat wound by applying a cotton pack.

Heat stroke
Submerge dog in cold bath; cool down with fresh air and water; go to the vet.

Frostbite/Hypothermia
Warm the dog with a warm bath, electric blankets or hot water bottles.

Abrasions
Clean the wound and wash out thoroughly with fresh water; apply antiseptic.

 Remember: an injured dog may attempt to bite a helping hand from fear and confusion. Always muzzle the dog before trying to offer assistance.

The Australian Shepherd is an extremely adaptable dog that can fit into and be happy in almost any living situation, provided that proper care, training and exercise take place from puppyhood and throughout the dog's entire life.

DIETARY AND FEEDING CONSIDERATIONS

Initially, the type and brand of food you'll feed your Aussie should be the same as what he's been receiving in his birth or previous home. Expect to serve the same number of meals that he's been getting in the past. As the puppy grows, he may require fewer meals per day than he consumed in the growing stage. Make any food changes gradually, as suddenly changing diet or eating habits can cause intestinal problems and great discomfort to the dog.

Today the choices of food for your Aussie are many and varied. There are simply dozens of brands of food in all sorts of flavors and textures, ranging from puppy diets to those for seniors. There are even hypoallergenic and low-calorie diets available. Because your Aussie's food has a bearing on coat, health and temperament, it is essential that the most suitable diet is selected for an Aussie of his age. It is fair to say, however, that even experienced owners can be perplexed by the enormous range of foods available. Only understanding what is best for your dog will help you reach an informed decision.

Dog foods are produced in three basic types: dry, semi-moist and canned. Dry foods are useful

---

FOOD PREFERENCE

Selecting the best dry dog food is difficult. There is no majority consensus among veterinary scientists as to the value of nutrient analyses (protein, fat, fiber, moisture, ash, cholesterol, minerals, etc.). All agree that feeding trials are what matter, but you also have to consider the individual dog. The dog's weight, age and activity level, and what pleases his taste, all must be considered. It is probably best to take the advice of your veterinarian. Every dog's dietary requirements vary, even during the lifetime of a particular dog.

If your dog is fed a good dry food, it does not require supplements of meat or vegetables. Dogs do appreciate a little variety in their diets, so you may choose to stay with the same brand but vary the flavor. Alternatively, you may wish to add a little flavored stock to give a difference to the taste.

for the cost-conscious as they tend to be less expensive than semi-moist or canned. They also contain the least fat and the most preservatives. In general, canned foods are made up of 60–70% water, while semi-moist ones often contain so much sugar that they are perhaps the least preferred by owners, even though their dogs seem to like them.

When selecting your dog's diet, three stages of development must be considered: the puppy stage, the adult stage and the senior stage.

PUPPY STAGE

Puppies instinctively want to suck milk from their mother's teats and a normal puppy will exhibit this behavior from just a few moments following birth. If puppies do not attempt to suckle within the first half-hour or so, the breeder should encourage them to do so by placing them on the nipples, having selected ones with plenty of milk. This early milk supply is important in providing colostrum to protect the puppies during the first eight to ten weeks of their lives. Although a mother's milk is much better than any milk formula, despite there being some excellent ones available, if the puppies do not feed, the breeder will have to feed them himself. For those with less experience, advice from a veterinarian is important so that not only the

FOOD STORAGE
You must store your dry dog food carefully. Open packages of dog food quickly lose their vitamin value, usually within 90 days of being opened. Mold spores and vermin could also contaminate the food.

right quantity of milk is fed but also that of correct quality, fed at suitably frequent intervals, usually every two hours during the first few days of life.

Puppies should be allowed to nurse from their mothers for about the first six weeks, although from the third or fourth week the breeder should begin to introduce small portions of suitable solid food. Most breeders like to introduce alternate milk

An Aussie's dietary requirements change as the dog matures. Consult your veterinarian for advice as to when and how to change the diet, if necessary.

and meat meals initially, building up to weaning time.

By the time the puppies are seven or a maximum of eight weeks old, they should be fully weaned and fed solely on a

TEST FOR PROPER DIET

A good test for proper diet is the color, odor and firmness of your dog's stool. A healthy dog usually produces three semi-hard stools per day. The stools should have no unpleasant odor. They should be the same color from excretion to excretion. Any abnormalities should be reported to the vet.

proprietary puppy food. Selection of the most suitable, good-quality diet at this time is essential, for a puppy's fastest growth rate is during the first year of life. Veterinarians are usually able to offer advice in this regard and, although the frequency of meals will be reduced over time, only when a young dog has reached the age of about 10 to 12 months should an adult diet be fed.

Puppy and junior diets should be well balanced for the needs of your dog, so that except in certain circumstances additional vitamins, minerals and proteins will not be required.

ADULT DIETS

A dog is considered an adult when it has stopped growing, so in general the diet of an Aussie can be changed to an adult one at about 10 to 12 months of age. Again you should rely upon your veterinarian or dietary specialist to recommend an acceptable maintenance diet. Major dog-food manufacturers specialize in this type of food, and it is merely necessary for you to select the one best suited to your dog's needs. Active dogs have different requirements than sedate dogs.

SENIOR DIETS

As dogs get older, their metabolism changes. The older dog usually exercises less, moves more slowly and sleeps more. This change in lifestyle and physiological performance requires a change in diet. Since these changes take place slowly, they might not be recognizable. What is easily recognizable is weight gain. By continuing to feed your dog an adult-maintenance diet when it is slowing down metabolically, your dog will gain weight. Obesity in an older dog compounds the health problems that already accompany old age.

As your dog gets older, few of his organs function up to par. The kidneys slow down and the intestines become less efficient. These age-related factors are best handled with a change in diet and a change in feeding schedule to give smaller portions that are more easily digested.

There is no single best diet for every older dog. While many dogs do well on light or senior diets, other dogs do better on puppy diets or other special premium diets such as lamb and rice. Be sensitive to your senior Aussie's diet and this will help control other problems that may arise with your old friend.

FEEDING TIPS

Dog food must be served at room temperature, neither too hot nor too cold.

Fresh water, changed often and served in a clean bowl, is mandatory, especially when feeding dry food.

Never feed your dog from the table while you are eating, and never feed your dog leftovers from your own meal. They usually contain too much fat and too much seasoning.

Dogs must chew their food. Hard pellets are excellent; soups and stews are to be avoided.

Don't add leftovers or any extras to normal dog food. The normal food is usually balanced, and adding something extra destroys the balance.

Except for age-related changes, dogs do not require dietary variations. They can be fed the same diet, day after day, without becoming bored or ill.

A
Worthy
Investment

Veterinary studies have proven that a balanced high-quality diet
pays off in your dog's coat quality, behavior and activity level.
Invest in premium brands for the maximum benefit for your dog.

WATER

Just as your dog needs proper nutrition from his food, water is an essential "nutrient" as well. Water keeps the dog's body properly hydrated and promotes normal function of the body's systems. During housebreaking, it is necessary to keep an eye on how much water your Aussie is drinking, but once he is reliably trained he should have access to clean fresh water at all times, especially if you feed dry food. Make certain that the dog's water bowl is clean, and change the water often.

EXERCISE

All dogs require some form of exercise, regardless of breed. A

THE CANINE GOURMET

Your dog does not prefer a fresh bone. Indeed, he wants it properly aged and, if given such a treat indoors, he is more likely to try to bury it in the carpet than he is to settle in for a good chew! If you have a yard, give him such delicacies outside and guide him to a place suitable for his "bone yard." He will carefully place the treasure in its earthy vault and seemingly forget about it. His seeming distaste or lack of thanks for your thoughtfulness is not that at all. He will return in a few days to inspect the bone, perhaps to re-bury it, and when it is just right, he will relish it as much as you do that cooked-to-perfection steak. If he is in a concrete or bricked kennel run, he will be especially frustrated at the hopelessness of the situation. He will vacillate between ignoring it completely, giving it a few licks to speed the curing process with saliva and trying to hide it behind the water bowl! When the bone has aged a bit, he will set to work on it.

IDEAL WEIGHT

Many people believe that extra weight on their dogs is a good thing. The truth is, pets should not be over- or underweight, as both can lead to or signal sickness. In order to tell how fit your pet is, run your hands over his ribs. Are his ribs buried under a layer of fat or are they sticking out considerably? If your pet is within his normal weight range, you should be able to feel the ribs easily, but they should not protrude abnormally. If you stand above him, the outline of his body should resemble an hourglass. Some breeds do tend to be leaner while some are a bit stockier, but making sure your dog is the right weight for his breed will certainly contribute to his good health.

sedentary lifestyle is as harmful to a dog as it is to a person. Throughout this book, emphasis has been placed on Aussie activity. The breed is an active one that must be kept busy and active throughout their lives. A casual stroll around the neighborhood once a day isn't sufficient exercise for the Aussie.

While very young puppies usually get adequate amounts of

DRINK, DRANK, DRUNK—MAKE IT A DOUBLE

In both humans and dogs, as well as most other living organisms, water forms the major part of nearly every body tissue. Naturally, we take water for granted, but without it, life as we know it would cease.

For dogs, water is needed to keep their bodies functioning biochemically. Additionally, water is needed to replace the water lost while panting. Unlike humans, who are able to sweat to dissipate heat, dogs must pant to cool down, thereby losing the vital water from their bodies needed to regulate their body temperatures. Humans lose electrolyte-containing products and other body-fluid components through sweating; dogs do not lose anything except water.

Water is essential always, but especially so when the weather is hot or humid or when your dog is exercising or working vigorously.

exercise by just moving around the house with you, that stage of life quickly comes to a halt. As the puppy reaches adolescence, his need for physical activity increases dramatically.

Playing in the yard, long brisk walks and running games all help build his muscles while preparing the adolescent's body for the strenuous life of a working dog. The fact that he may not be destined for ranch work and herding cattle does not diminish the need for physical stimulation.

Again, ideally you purchased your Aussie because you want to have a working dog to help you on your ranch or because your lifestyle includes many outdoor activities. Either way, you should make that puppy a part of your busy lifestyle as soon as possible once he is past the baby stage. He will love being with you, working with you and pleasing you. This is his destiny and his Aussie heritage is just waiting to be revealed to a loving, caring owner like you.

While the Aussie is an active breed that enjoys exercise, you don't have to be an Olympic athlete to keep up with your dog. Regular walks, play sessions in the yard and letting the dog run free in the yard under your supervision are great exercise for the Aussie. For those who are more ambitious, you will find that your Aussie also enjoys long walks, an occasional hike, games of fetch or even a swim! Bear in mind that an overweight dog should never be suddenly over-exercised; instead, he should be encouraged to increase exercise slowly. Not only is exercise essential to keep the dog's body fit, it is essential to his mental well-being. A bored dog will find something to do, which often manifests itself in some type of destructive behavior. In this sense, exercise is essential for the owner's mental well-being as well!

GROOMING

Aussies require only a minimum amount of grooming if they are brushed on a regular schedule, say every other day. The dog

that spends a lot of time outdoors will likely pick up more foreign matter in his coat than the one that spends most of his time indoors. Regular grooming sessions are a good way to spend time with your dog. Many dogs grow to like the feel of being brushed and will enjoy the regular routine.

Cleaning your Aussie's teeth can be done on a regular basis by you at home. However, your veterinarian should teach you the correct procedure and should also supply you with the proper supplies for dental hygiene.

Given an open space in which to run and perhaps a favorite toy, Aussies have no trouble providing themselves with exercise. You, however, must provide your dog with supervision.

BATHING

Dogs do not need to be bathed as often as humans, but regular bathing is essential for healthy skin and a shiny coat. Again, like most anything, if you accustom your pup to being bathed as a

---

THAT'S ENTERTAINMENT!

Is your dog home alone for much of the day? If you haven't taught him how to crochet or play the French horn, then he'll probably need something to occupy his paws and jaws, lest he turn to chewing up the carpet and draperies. Recommended conditioning devices are toys that stimulate your dog both physically and mentally. Some of the most popular toys are those that are constructed to hide food inside. They provide not only a challenge but also instant gratification when your dog gets to the treat. Be sure to clean these carefully to prevent bacteria from building up.

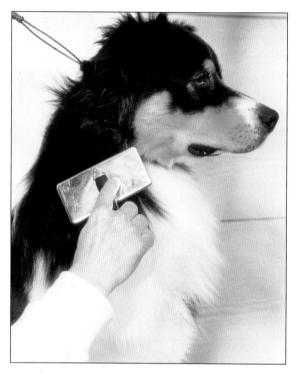

puppy, it will become second nature by the time he grows up. You want your dog to be at ease in the bath or else it could end up a wet, soapy, messy ordeal for both of you! Bathing your Aussie will probably be necessary several times a year, but not too often as shampooing removes essential oils from his coat. Always use a dog shampoo because human shampoos dry out the coat too much and can cause skin irritation.

Brush your Aussie thoroughly before wetting his coat. This will get rid of most mats and tangles, which are harder to remove when the coat is wet. Make certain that your dog has a good non-slip surface to stand on.

Brushing is a simple matter if your Aussie is accustomed to it; many dogs even grow to like the feeling of being brushed.

Regularly combing all areas of your Aussie's coat is necessary to remove tangles and debris and to prevent mats from forming.

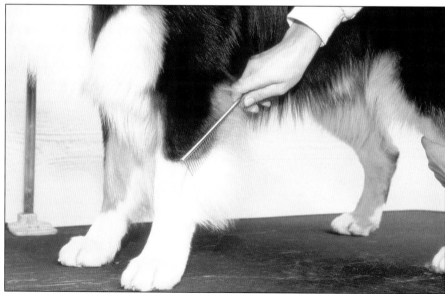

GROOMING EQUIPMENT

How much grooming equipment you purchase will depend on how much grooming you are going to do. Here are some basics:

- Natural bristle brush
- Slicker brush
- Metal comb
- Blow dryer
- Rubber mat
- Dog shampoo
- Spray hose attachment
- Ear cleaner
- Cotton balls
- Towels
- Nail clippers
- Dental-care supplies

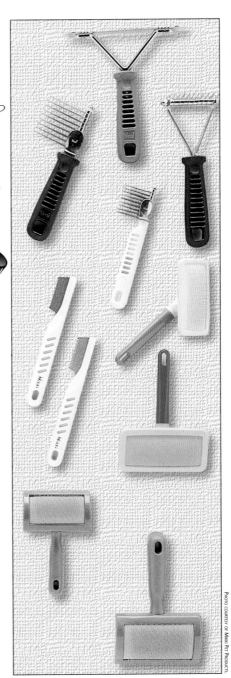

Your local pet shop should have a variety of grooming tools from which you can select brushes and combs for maintaining your Aussie's coat.

Wet the coat thoroughly and apply shampoo. Wash the head last; you do not want shampoo to drip into the dog's eyes while you are washing the rest of his body. Work the shampoo all the way down to the skin. You can use this opportunity to check the skin for any bumps, bites or other abnormalities. Do not neglect any area of the body—get all of the hard-to-reach places.

While you're in the process of bathing your Aussie, lift each ear flap and gently wipe the inside of the ears with a damp cloth. Never force your finger or any object down into the deeper part of the ear. Wipe only the surface that you can see and touch easily. Any further clean-

SOAP IT UP

The use of human soap products like shampoo, bubble bath and hand soap can be damaging to a dog's coat and skin. Human products are too strong; they remove the protective oils coating the dog's hair and skin that make him water-resistant. Use only shampoo made especially for dogs. You may like to use a medicated shampoo, which will help to keep external parasites at bay and is soothing to the dog's skin as well.

The Aussie's long coat can pick up burrs and foreign objects in the grass. Brush him out after play sessions in the grass.

ing must be done by your veterinarian.

The ears should be kept clean with a cotton ball and ear powder made especially for dogs. Be on the lookout for any signs of infection or ear-mite infestation. If your Aussie has been shaking

his head or scratching at his ears frequently, this usually indicates a problem. If his ears have an unusual odor, this is a sure sign of mite infestation or infection, and a signal to have his ears checked by the veterinarian.

Once the dog has been thoroughly shampooed, he requires an equally thorough rinsing. Shampoo left in the coat can be irritating to the skin. Protect his eyes from the shampoo by shielding them with your hand and directing the flow of water in the opposite direction. You should also avoid getting water in the ear canal. Then towel dry the dog by briskly rubbing him all over. Be

BATHING BEAUTY

Once you are sure that the dog is thoroughly rinsed, squeeze the excess water out of his coat with your hand and dry him with a heavy towel. You may choose to use a blow dryer on his coat or just let it dry naturally. In cold weather, never allow your dog outside with a wet coat. A dog with a damp coat is extremely susceptible to catching a cold.

There are "dry bath" products on the market, which are sprays and powders intended for spot cleaning that can be used between regular baths if necessary. They are not substitutes for regular baths, but they are easy to use for touch-ups as they do not require rinsing. These are ideal in the winter months.

prepared for your dog to shake out his coat—you might want to stand back, but make sure you have a hold on the dog to keep him from running through the house. If you wish to use a blow dryer, be sure it is set on the lowest temperature so as not to burn the dog. Keep the dog out of cold air and drafts until he's completely dry.

NAIL CLIPPING

Your Aussie should be accustomed to having his nails trimmed at an early age, since it will be part of your maintenance routine throughout his life. Not only does it look nicer, but long nails can scratch someone unintentionally. Also, a long nail has a better chance of ripping and bleeding, or causing the feet to spread. A good rule of thumb is that if you can hear your dog's nails' clicking on the floor when he walks, his nails are too long.

Before you start cutting, make sure you can identify the "quick" in each nail. The quick is a blood vessel that runs through the center of each nail and grows rather close to the end. It will bleed if accidentally cut, which will be quite painful for the dog as it contains nerve endings.

Keep some type of clotting agent on hand, such as a styptic pencil or styptic powder (the type used for shaving). This will

PEDICURE TIP

A dog that spends a lot of time outside on a hard surface, such as cement or pavement, will have his nails naturally worn down and may not need to have them trimmed as often, except maybe in the colder months when he is not outside as much. Regardless, it is best to get your dog accustomed to the nail-trimming procedure at an early age so that he is used to it. Some dogs are especially sensitive about having their feet touched, but if a dog has experienced it since puppyhood, it should not bother him.

stop the bleeding quickly when applied to the end of the cut nail. Do not panic if you cut the quick, just stop the bleeding and talk soothingly to your dog. Once he has calmed down, move on to the next nail. It is better to clip a little at a time, particularly with black-nailed dogs.

Hold your pup steady as you begin trimming his nails; you do not want him to make any

EXERCISE ALERT!

You should be careful where you exercise your dog or where you let him explore, especially in unfamiliar areas. Many countryside areas have been sprayed with chemicals that are highly toxic to both dogs and humans. Never allow your dog to eat grass or drink from puddles on either public or private grounds, as the run-off water may contain chemicals from sprays and herbicides.

sudden movements or run away. Talk to him soothingly and stroke him as you clip. Holding his foot in your hand, simply take off the end of each nail in one quick clip. You can purchase nail clippers that are specially made for dogs; you can probably find them wherever you buy grooming supplies.

TRAVELING WITH YOUR DOG

Car Travel

You should accustom your Aussie to riding in a car at an early age. You may or may not take him in the car often, but at the very least he will need to go to the vet and you do not want these trips to be traumatic for the dog or troublesome for you. The safest way for a dog to ride in the car is in his crate. If he uses a crate in the house, you can use the same crate for travel.

Put the pup in the crate and see how he reacts. If he seems uneasy, you can have a passenger hold him on his lap while you drive. Another option is a specially made safety harness for dogs, which straps the dog in much like a seat belt. Do not let the dog roam loose in the vehicle—this is very dangerous! If you should stop short, your dog can be thrown and injured. If the dog starts climbing on you and pestering you while you are driving, you will not be able to concentrate on the road. It is an unsafe situation for everyone—human and canine.

For long trips, be prepared to stop to let the dog relieve himself. Take with you whatever you need to clean up after him, including some paper towels and perhaps some old bath towels for use should he have an accident in the car or suffer from motion sickness.

AIR TRAVEL

Airlines have different requirements pertaining to transporting pets. Always contact your chosen airline well beforehand. The dog will be required to travel in a fiberglass crate and you should always check in advance with the airline about specific requirements regarding crate size, type and labeling. To help the dog be at ease, put one of his favorite toys in the crate with him. You must feed the dog within four hours of check-in, but a light meal is best; do not overfeed. Certain regulations specify that water and food bowls must be attached to the crate.

Make sure your dog is properly identified and that your contact information appears on his ID tags and on his crate. Animals travel in a different area of the plane than human passengers, so every rule must be strictly followed so as to prevent the risk of getting separated from your dog.

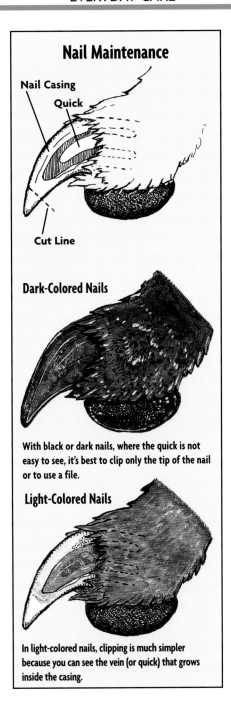

Nail Maintenance

Nail Casing

Quick

Cut Line

Dark-Colored Nails

With black or dark nails, where the quick is not easy to see, it's best to clip only the tip of the nail or to use a file.

Light-Colored Nails

In light-colored nails, clipping is much simpler because you can see the vein (or quick) that grows inside the casing.

TRAVEL TIP

Never leave your dog alone in the car. In hot weather, your dog can die from the high temperature inside a closed vehicle; even a car parked in the shade can heat up very quickly. Leaving the window open is dangerous as well since the dog can hurt himself trying to get out.

Aussies like to be involved in their owners everyday lives, but they look forward to vacations the most!

BOARDING AND VACATIONS

So you want to take a family vacation—and you want to include *all* members of the family. You would probably make arrangements for accommodations ahead of time anyway, but this is especially important when traveling with a dog. You do not want to make an overnight stop at the only place around for miles and find out that they do not allow dogs. Also, you do not want to reserve a place for your family without confirming that you are traveling with a dog, because if it is against their policy you may not have a place to stay.

Alternatively, if you are traveling and choose not to bring your Aussie, you will have to make arrangements for him while you are away. Some options are to take him to a neighbor's house to stay while you are gone, to have a trusted neighbor drop by often or stay at your house or to bring your dog to a reputable boarding kennel. If you choose to board him at a kennel, you should visit in advance to see the facilities provided, how clean they are and where the dogs are kept. Talk to some of the employees and see how they treat the dogs—do they spend time with the dogs, play with them, exercise them, etc.? Also find out the kennel's policy on vaccinations and what they require. This is for all of the dogs' safety, since when dogs are kept together, there is a greater risk of diseases being passed from dog to dog.

IDENTIFICATION OPTIONS

As puppies become more and more expensive, especially those puppies of high quality for showing and/or breeding, they have a greater chance of being stolen. The usual collar dog tag is, of course, easily removed. But there are two more permanent techniques that have become widely used for identification.

The puppy microchip implantation involves the injection of a small microchip, about the size of a corn kernel, under the skin of the dog. If your dog shows up at a clinic or shelter, or is offered for resale under less-than-savory circumstances, it can be positively identified by the microchip. The microchip is scanned, and a registry quickly identifies you as the owner.

Tattooing is done on various parts of the dog, from his belly to his cheeks. The number tattooed can be your telephone number or any other number that you can easily memorize. When professional dog thieves see a tattooed dog, they usually lose interest. Both microchipping and tattooing can be done at your local veterinary clinic. For the safety of our dogs, no laboratory facility or dog broker will accept a tattooed dog as stock.

IDENTIFICATION

Your Aussie is your valued companion and friend. That is why you always keep a close eye on him and you have made sure that he cannot escape from the yard or wriggle out of his collar and run away from you. However, accidents can happen and there may come a time when your dog unexpectedly gets separated from you. If this unfortunate event should occur, the first thing on your mind will be finding him. Proper identification, including an ID tag, a tattoo and possibly a microchip, will increase the chances of his being returned to you safely and quickly.

Whenever your Aussie is outdoors, be certain that he is outfitted with his collar and ID tag.

Living with an untrained dog is a lot like owning a piano that you do not know how to play—it is a nice object to look at, but it does not do much more than that to bring you pleasure. Now try taking piano lessons, and suddenly the piano comes alive and brings forth magical sounds and rhythms that set your heart singing and your body swaying.

The same is true with your Australian Shepherd. Any dog is a big responsibility and if not trained sensibly may develop unacceptable behavior that annoys you or could even cause family friction.

To train your Aussie, you may like to enroll in an obedience class. Teach him good manners as you learn how and why he behaves the way he does. Find out how to communicate with your dog and how to recognize and understand his communications with you. Suddenly the dog takes on a new role in your life—he is clever, interesting, well behaved and fun to be with. He demonstrates his bond of devotion to you daily. In other words, your Aussie does wonders for your ego because he constantly reminds you that you are not only his leader, you are his hero!

PARENTAL GUIDANCE

Training a dog is a life experience. Many parents admit that much of what they know about raising children they learned from caring for their dogs. Dogs respond to love, fairness and guidance, just as children do. Don't spoil or mistreat your Aussie. Become a good dog owner and you may become an even better parent.

Those involved with teaching dog obedience and counseling owners about their dogs' behavior have discovered some interesting facts about dog ownership. For example, training dogs when they are puppies results in the highest rate of success in developing well-mannered and well-adjusted adult dogs. Training an older dog, from six months to six years of age, can produce almost equal results, providing that the owner accepts the dog's slower rate of learning capability and is willing to work patiently to help the dog succeed at developing to his fullest potential. Unfortunately, many owners of untrained adult dogs lack the patience factor, so they do not persist until their dogs are successful at learning particular behaviors.

Training a puppy aged 10 to 16 weeks (20 weeks at the most) is like working with a dry sponge in a pool of water. The pup soaks up whatever you show him and constantly looks for more things to do and learn. At this early age, his body is not yet producing hormones, and therein lies the reason for such a high rate of success. Without hormones, he is focused on his owners and not particularly interested in investigating other places, dogs, people, etc. You are his leader: his provider of food, water, shelter and security. He

HONOR AND OBEY
Most animal behaviorists and all dog owners agree that dogs are the most honorable animals in existence. They consider another species (humans) as their own. They interface with you. You are their leader. Puppies perceive children to be on their level; their actions around small children are different from their behavior around their adult masters.

latches onto you and wants to stay close. He will usually follow you from room to room, will not let you out of his sight when you are outdoors with him and will respond in like manner to the people and animals you encounter. If you greet a friend warmly, he will be happy to greet the person as well. If, however, you are hesitant, even anxious,

> ## THINK BEFORE YOU BARK
> Dogs are sensitive to their masters' moods and emotions. Aussies instinctively sense when their owners are happy, preoccupied, upset or nervous. Relay your intentions to your dog clearly through vocal commands. Use your voice wisely—never raise your voice at your dog unless you are trying to correct him. "Barking" at your dog can become as meaningless as "dogspeak" is to you.

classes lies within the pages of this book.

This chapter is devoted to helping you train your Aussie at home. If the recommended procedures are followed faithfully, you may expect positive results that will prove rewarding both to you and your dog.

Whether your new charge is a puppy or a mature adult, the methods of teaching and the techniques we use in training basic behaviors are the same. After all, no dog, whether puppy or adult, likes harsh or inhumane methods. All creatures, however, respond favorably to gentle motivational methods and sincere praise and encouragement. Now let us get started.

about the approach of a stranger, he will respond accordingly.

Once the puppy begins to produce hormones, his natural curiosity emerges and he begins to investigate the world around him. It is at this time when you may notice that the untrained dog begins to wander away from you and even ignore your commands to stay close. When this behavior becomes a problem, the owner has two choices: get rid of the dog or train him. It is strongly urged that you choose the latter option.

There are usually classes within a reasonable distance from the owner's home, but you can also do a lot to train your dog yourself. Sometimes there are classes available but the tuition is too costly. Whatever the circumstances, the solution to the problem of training your Aussie without formal obedience

HOUSE-TRAINING
You can train a puppy to relieve himself wherever you choose, but this must be somewhere suitable. You should bear in mind from the outset that when your

> ## HIS OWN LITTLE CORNER
> Mealtime should be a peaceful time for your puppy. Do not put his food and water bowls in a high-traffic area in the house. For example, give him his own little corner of the kitchen where he can eat undisturbed and where he will not be underfoot. Do not allow small children or other family members to disturb the pup when he is eating.

Aussies are extremely intelligent dogs; they are probably one of the most intelligent of all dog breeds. Consequently, they master commands quickly. Here, the Aussie and handler demonstrate off-lead heeling, which is an advanced obedience exercise.

puppy is old enough to go out in public places, any canine deposits must be removed at once. You will always have to carry with you a small plastic bag or "poop-scoop."

REAP THE REWARDS

If you start with a normal, healthy dog and give him time, patience and some carefully executed lessons, you will reap the rewards of that training for the life of the dog. And what a life it will be! The two of you will find immeasurable pleasure in the companionship you have built together with a bond of love, respect and understanding.

Outdoor training includes such surfaces as grass, soil and cement. Indoor training usually means training your dog to newspaper.

When deciding on the surface and location that you will want your Aussie to use, be sure it is going to be permanent. Training your dog to grass and then changing your mind two months later is extremely difficult for both dog and owner.

Next, choose the command you will use each and every time you want your puppy to void. "Hurry up" and "Go potty" are examples of commands commonly used by dog owners.

Get in the habit of giving the puppy your chosen relief command before you take him out. That way, when he becomes an adult, you will be able to determine if he wants to go out when you ask him. A confirmation will be signs of interest, such as wagging his tail, watching you intently, going to the door, etc.

PUPPY'S NEEDS

The puppy needs to relieve himself after play periods, after each meal, after he has been sleeping and at any time he indicates that he is looking for a place to urinate or defecate.

The urinary and intestinal tract muscles of very young puppies are not fully developed.

Therefore, like human babies, puppies need to relieve themselves frequently.

Take your puppy out often—every hour for an eight-week-old, for example, and always immediately after sleeping and eating. The older the puppy, the less often he will need to relieve himself. Finally, as a mature healthy adult, he will require only three to five relief trips per day.

HOUSING

Since the types of housing and control you provide for your puppy have a direct relationship on the success of house-training, we consider the various aspects of both before we begin training.

Taking a new puppy home and turning him loose in your house can be compared to turning a child loose in a sports arena and telling the child that the place is all his! The sheer enormity of the place would be too much for him to handle.

Instead, offer the puppy clearly defined areas where he can play, sleep, eat and live. A room of the house where the family gathers is the most obvious choice. Puppies are social animals and need to feel a part of the pack right from the start. Hearing your voice, watching you while you are doing things and smelling you nearby are all positive reinforcers that he is

TRAINING TIP
Dogs will do anything for your attention. If you reward the dog when he is calm and attentive, you will develop a well-mannered dog. If, on the other hand, you greet your dog excitedly and encourage him to wrestle with you, the dog will greet you the same way and you will have a hyperactive dog on your hands.

now a member of your pack. Usually a family room, the kitchen or a nearby adjoining breakfast area is ideal for provid-

TAKE THE LEAD
Do not carry your dog to his relief area. Lead him there on a leash or, better yet, encourage him to follow you to the spot. If you start carrying him to his spot, you might end up doing this routine forever and your dog will have the satisfaction of having trained you.

ing safety and security for both puppy and owner.

Within that room there should be a smaller area that the puppy can call his own. An alcove, a wire or fiberglass dog crate or a fenced (not boarded!) corner from which he can view the activities of his new family will be fine. The size of the area or crate is the key factor here. The area must be large enough for the puppy to lie down and stretch out as well as stand up without rubbing his head on the top, yet small enough so that he cannot relieve himself at one end and sleep at the other without coming into contact with his droppings before he is fully trained to relieve himself outside.

Dogs are, by nature, clean animals and will not remain close to their relief areas unless forced to do so. In those cases, they then become dirty dogs and usually remain that way for life.

The designated area should contain clean bedding and a toy.

Water must always be available, in a non-spill container.

CONTROL
By control, we mean helping the puppy to create a lifestyle pattern that will be compatible to that of his human pack (YOU!). Just as we guide little children to learn our way of life, we must show the puppy when it is time to play, eat, sleep, exercise and even entertain himself.

Your puppy should always sleep in his crate. He should also learn that, during times of household confusion and excessive human activity such as at breakfast when family members are preparing for the day, he can play by himself in relative safety and comfort in his designated area. Each time you leave the puppy alone, he should under-

PAPER CAPER
Never line your pup's sleeping area with newspaper. Puppy litters are usually raised on newspaper and, once in your home, the puppy will immediately associate newspaper with voiding. Never put newspaper on any floor while house-training, as this will only confuse the puppy. If you are paper-training him, use paper in his designated relief area only. Finally, restrict water intake after evening meals. Offer a few licks at a time—never let a young puppy gulp water after meals.

CANINE DEVELOPMENT SCHEDULE

It is important to understand how and at what age a puppy develops into adulthood. If you are a puppy owner, consult the following Canine Development Schedule to determine the stage of development your puppy is currently experiencing. This knowledge will help you as you work with the puppy in the weeks and months ahead.

Period	Age	Characteristics
FIRST TO THIRD	BIRTH TO SEVEN WEEKS	Puppy needs food, sleep and warmth, and responds to simple and gentle touching. Needs mother for security and disciplining. Needs littermates for learning and interacting with other dogs. Pup learns to function within a pack and learns pack order of dominance. Begin socializing with adults and children for short periods. Begins to become aware of its environment.
FOURTH	EIGHT TO TWELVE WEEKS	Brain is fully developed. Needs socializing with outside world. Remove from mother and littermates. Needs to change from canine pack to human pack. Human dominance necessary. Fear period occurs between 8 and 10 weeks. Avoid fright and pain.
FIFTH	THIRTEEN TO SIXTEEN WEEKS	Training and formal obedience should begin. Less association with other dogs, more with people, places, situations. Period will pass easily if you remember this is pup's change-to-adolescence time. Be firm and fair. Flight instinct prominent. Permissiveness and over-disciplining can do permanent damage. Praise for good behavior.
JUVENILE	FOUR TO EIGHT MONTHS	Another fear period about 7 to 8 months of age. It passes quickly, but be cautious of fright and pain. Sexual maturity reached. Dominant traits established. Dog should understand sit, down, come and stay by now.

NOTE: THESE ARE APPROXIMATE TIME FRAMES. ALLOW FOR INDIVIDUAL DIFFERENCES IN PUPPIES.

stand exactly where he is to stay. Puppies are chewers. They cannot tell the difference between lamp cords, television wires, shoes, table legs, etc. Chewing into a television wire, for example, can be fatal to the puppy, while a shorted wire can start a fire in the house.

If the puppy chews on the arm of the chair when he is alone, you will probably discipline him angrily when you get

THE SUCCESS METHOD

Success that comes by luck is usually short-lived. Success that comes by well-thought-out proven methods is often more easily achieved and permanent. This is the Success Method. It is designed to give you, the puppy owner, a simple yet proven way to help your puppy develop clean living habits and a feeling of security in his new environment.

6 Steps to Successful Crate Training

1 Tell the puppy "Crate time!" and place him in the crate with a small treat (a piece of cheese or half of a biscuit). Let him stay in the crate for five minutes while you are in the same room. Then release him and praise lavishly. Never release him when he is fussing. Wait until he is quiet before you let him out.

2 Repeat Step 1 several times a day.

3 The next day, place the puppy in the crate as before. Let him stay there for ten minutes. Do this several times.

4 Continue building time in five-minute increments until the puppy stays in his crate for 30 minutes with you in the room. Always take him to his relief area after prolonged periods in his crate.

5 Now go back to Step 1 and let the puppy stay in his crate for five minutes, this time while you are out of the room.

6 Once again, build crate time in five-minute increments with you out of the room. When the puppy will stay willingly in his crate (he may even fall asleep!) for 30 minutes with you out of the room, he will be ready to stay in it for several hours at a time.

home. Thus, he makes the association that your coming home means he is going to be punished. (He will not remember chewing the chair and is incapable of making the association of the discipline with his naughty deed.)

Other times of excitement, such as family parties, etc., can be fun for the puppy, providing he can view the activities from the security of his designated area. He is not underfoot and he is not being fed all sorts of

THE CLEAN LIFE

By providing sleeping and resting quarters that fit the dog, and offering frequent opportunities to relieve himself outside his quarters, the puppy quickly learns that the outdoors (or the newspaper if you are training him to paper) is the place to go when he needs to urinate or defecate. It also reinforces his innate desire to keep his sleeping quarters clean. This, in turn, helps develop the muscle control that will eventually produce a dog with clean living habits.

Always clean up after your Aussie, whether you are in a public place or your own yard.

tidbits that will probably cause him stomach distress, yet he still feels a part of the fun.

SCHEDULE

A puppy should be taken to his relief area each time he is released from his designated area, after meals, after a play session and when he first awakens in the morning (at age eight weeks, this can mean 5 a.m.!). The puppy will indicate that he's ready "to go" by circling or sniffing busily—do not misinterpret these signs. For a puppy less than ten weeks of age, a routine of taking him out every hour is necessary. As the puppy grows, he will be able to wait for longer periods of time.

Keep trips to his relief area short. Stay no more than five or six minutes and then return to the

HOW MANY TIMES A DAY?

AGE	RELIEF TRIPS
To 14 weeks	10
14–22 weeks	8
22–32 weeks	6
Adulthood (dog stops growing)	4

These are estimates, of course, but they are a guide to the minimum number of opportunities a dog should have each day to relieve itself.

The schedule you determine for your Aussie puppy will become the basis of your dog's routine for life.

HOUSE-TRAINING TIP
Most of all, be consistent. Always take your dog to the same location, always use the same command and always have the dog on lead when he is in his relief area, unless a fenced-in yard is available.

Once indoors, put the puppy in his crate until you have had time to clean up his accident. Then release him to the family area and watch him more closely than before. Chances are, his accident was a result of your not picking up his signal or waiting too long before offering him the opportunity to relieve himself. Never hold a grudge against the puppy for accidents.

house. If he goes during that time, praise him lavishly and take him indoors immediately. If he does not, but he has an accident when you go back indoors, pick him up immediately, say "No! No!" and return to his relief area. Wait a few minutes, then return to the house again. Never hit a puppy or rub his face in urine or excrement when he has had an accident!

Puppies are easily distracted from the lesson at hand. Each pup needs individual attention to cater to his needs.

Let the puppy learn that going outdoors means it is time to relieve himself, not play. Once trained, he will be able to play indoors and out and still differentiate between the times for play versus the times for relief.

Help him develop regular hours for naps, being alone, playing by himself and just resting, all in his crate. Encourage him to entertain himself while you are busy with your activities. Let him learn that having you near is comforting, but it is not your main purpose in life to provide him with undivided attention.

Each time you put a puppy in his own area, use the same command, whatever suits best. Soon he will run to his crate or special area when he hears you say those words.

Crate training provides safety for you, the puppy and the home. It also provides the puppy with a feeling of security, and that helps the puppy achieve self-confidence and clean habits.

Remember that one of the primary ingredients in house-training your puppy is control. Regardless of your lifestyle, there will always be occasions when you will need to have a place where your dog can stay and be happy and safe. Crate training is the answer for now and in the future.

In conclusion, a few key elements are really all you need for a successful house-training method—consistency, frequency, praise, control and supervision. By following these procedures with a normal, healthy puppy, you and the puppy will soon be past the stage of "accidents" and ready to move on to a full and rewarding life together.

PLAN TO PLAY

Both puppies and adult dogs should also have regular play and exercise sessions when he is with you or a family member. Exercise for a very young puppy can consist of a short walk around the house or yard. Playing can include fetching games with a large ball or a special toy. (All puppies teethe and need soft things upon which to chew.) Remember to restrict play periods to indoors within his living area (the family room, for example) until he is completely house-trained.

TRAINING RULES

If you want to be successful in training your dog, you have four rules to obey yourself:
1. Develop an understanding of how a dog thinks.
2. Do not blame the dog for lack of communication.
3. Define your dog's personality and act accordingly.
4. Have patience and be consistent.

ROLES OF DISCIPLINE, REWARD AND PUNISHMENT

Discipline, training one to act in accordance with rules, brings order to life. It is as simple as that. Without discipline, particularly in a group society, chaos reigns supreme and the group will eventually perish. Humans and canines are social animals and need some form of discipline in order to function effectively. They must procure food, protect their home base and their young and reproduce to keep the species going.

If there were no discipline in the lives of social animals, they would eventually die from starvation and/or predation by other stronger animals.

In the case of domestic canines, dogs need discipline in their lives in order to understand how their pack (you and other family members) functions and how they must act in order to survive.

A large humane society in a highly populated area recently surveyed dog owners regarding their satisfaction with their relationships with their dogs. People who had trained their dogs were 75% more satisfied with their pets than those who had never trained their dogs.

Dr. Edward Thorndike, a psychologist, established *Thorndike's Theory of Learning*, which states that a behavior that results in a pleasant event tends to be repeated. Likewise, a behavior that results in an unpleasant event tends not to be repeated. It is this theory on which training methods are based today. For example, if you manipulate a dog to perform a specific behavior and reward him for doing it, he is likely to do it again because he enjoyed the end result.

Occasionally, punishment, a penalty inflicted for an offense, is necessary. The best type of punishment often comes from an outside source. For example, a child is told not to touch the stove because he may get burned. He disobeys and touches the stove. In doing so, he receives a burn. From that time on, he respects the heat of the stove and avoids contact with it. Therefore, a behavior that results in an unpleasant event tends not to be repeated.

A good example of a dog learning the hard way is the dog who chases the house cat. He is told many times to leave the cat alone, yet he persists in teasing the cat. Then, one day he begins chasing the cat but the cat turns and swipes a claw across the dog's face, leaving him with a painful gash on his nose. The final result is that the dog stops chasing the cat.

TRAINING EQUIPMENT

COLLAR AND LEASH
For an Aussie, the collar and leash that you use for training must be one with which you are easily able to work, not too heavy for the dog and perfectly safe.

TREATS
Have a bag of treats on hand. Something nutritious and easy to

KEEP SMILING

Never train your dog, puppy or adult, when you are angry or in a sour mood. Dogs are very sensitive to human feelings, especially anger, and if your dog senses that you are angry or upset, he will connect your anger with his training and learn to resent or fear his training sessions.

COMMAND STANCE
Stand up straight and authoritatively when giving your dog commands. Do not issue commands when lying on the floor or lying on your back on the sofa. If you are on your hands and knees when you give a command, your dog will think you are positioning yourself to play.

swallow works best. Use a soft treat, a chunk of cheese or a piece of cooked chicken rather than a dry biscuit. By the time the dog has finished chewing a dry treat, he will forget why he is being rewarded in the first place! Using food rewards will not teach a dog to beg at the table—the only way to teach a dog to beg at the table is to give him food from the table. In training, rewarding the dog with a food treat will help him associate praise and the treats with learning new behaviors that obviously please his owner.

TRAINING BEGINS: ASK THE DOG A QUESTION
In order to teach your dog anything, you must first get his attention. After all, he cannot learn anything if he is looking away from you with his mind on something else.

To get his attention, ask him "School?" and immediately walk over to him and give him a treat as you tell him "Good dog." Wait a minute or two and repeat the routine, this time with a treat in your hand as you approach within a foot of the dog. Do not go directly to him, but stop about a foot short of him and hold out the treat as you ask "School?" He will see you approaching with a treat in your hand and most likely begin walking toward you. As you meet, give him the treat and praise again.

The third time, ask the question, have a treat in your hand and walk only a short distance toward the dog so that he must walk almost all the way to you. As he reaches you, give him the treat and praise again.

By this time, the dog will probably be getting the idea that if he pays attention to you, especially when you ask that question, it will pay off in treats and enjoyable activities for him. In other words, he learns that "school" means doing great things with you that are fun and result in positive attention for him.

Remember that the dog does not understand your verbal language; he only recognizes sounds. Your question translates to a series of sounds for him, and those sounds become the signal to go to you and pay attention; if he does, he will get to interact with you plus receive treats and praise.

THE BASIC COMMANDS

TEACHING SIT

Now that you have the dog's attention, attach his leash and hold it in your left hand and a food treat in your right. Place your food hand at the dog's nose and let him lick the treat but not take it from you. Say "Sit" and slowly raise your food hand from in front of the dog's nose up over his head so that he is looking at the ceiling. As he bends his head upward, he will have to bend his knees to maintain his balance. As he bends his knees, he will assume a sit position. At that point, release the food treat and praise lavishly with comments such as "Good dog! Good sit!," etc. Remember to always praise enthusiastically, because dogs relish verbal praise from their owners and feel so proud of themselves whenever they accomplish a behavior.

You will not use food forever in getting the dog to obey your commands. Food is only used to teach new behaviors, and once the dog knows what you want when you give a specific command, you will wean him off the food treats but still maintain the verbal praise. After all, you will always have your voice with you, and there will be many times when you have no food rewards but expect the dog to obey.

PRACTICE MAKES PERFECT!

In order for your Aussie to become a well-trained canine citizen, you must engage in a positive routine for his lessons. Dogs respond to *positive* reinforcement, so always make lessons a happy, rewarding experience.

- Have training lessons with your dog every day in several short segments—three to five times a day for a few minutes at a time is ideal.
- Do not have long practice sessions. The dog will become easily bored.
- Never practice when you are tired, ill, worried or in an otherwise negative mood. This will transmit to the dog and may have an adverse effect on its performance.

Think fun, short and above all positive! End each session on a high note, and make sure to give a lot of praise. Enjoy the training and help your dog enjoy it, too.

TEACHING DOWN

Teaching the down exercise is easy when you understand how the dog perceives the down position, and it is very difficult when you do not. Dogs perceive the down position as a submissive one; therefore, teaching the down exercise using a forceful method can sometimes make the dog develop such a fear of the down that he either runs away when you say "Down" or he attempts to snap at the person who tries to force him down.

Teaching the sit exercise is one of the easiest and first commands you will teach your Australian Shepherd.

Have the dog sit close alongside your left leg, facing in the same direction as you are. Hold the leash in your left hand and a food treat in your right. Now place your left hand lightly on the top of the dog's shoulders where they meet above the spinal cord. Do not push down on the dog's shoulders; simply rest your left hand there so you can guide the dog to lie down close to your left leg rather than to swing away from your side when he drops.

Now place the food hand at the dog's nose, say "Down" very softly (almost a whisper) and slowly lower the food hand to the dog's front feet. When the food hand reaches the floor, begin moving it forward along the floor in front of the dog. Keep talking softly to the dog, saying things like, "Do you want this treat? You can do this, good dog." Your reassuring tone of voice will help calm the dog as he tries to follow the food hand in order to get the treat.

When the dog's elbows touch the floor, release the food and praise softly. Try to get the dog to maintain that down position for several seconds before you let him sit up again. The goal here is to get the dog to settle down and not feel threatened in the down position.

TEACHING STAY

It is easy to teach the dog to stay in either a sit or a down position.

Again, we use food and praise during the teaching process as we help the dog to understand exactly what it is that we are expecting him to do.

To teach the sit/stay, start with the dog sitting on your left side as before and hold the leash in your left hand. Have a food treat in your right hand and place your food hand at the dog's nose. Say "Stay" and step out on your right foot to stand directly in front of the dog, toe to toe, as he licks and nibbles the treat. Be sure to keep his head facing upward to maintain the sit position. Count to five and then swing around to stand next to the dog again with him on your left. As soon as you get back to the original position, release the food and praise lavishly.

To teach the down/stay, do the down as previously described. As soon as the dog lies down, say "Stay" and step out on your right foot just as you did in the sit/stay. Count to five and then return to stand beside the dog with him on your left side. Release the treat and praise as always.

Within a week or ten days, you can begin to add a bit of distance between you and your dog when you leave him. When you do, use your left hand open with the palm facing the dog as a stay signal, much the same as the hand signal a police officer uses

DOUBLE JEOPARDY

A dog in jeopardy never lies down. He stays alert on his feet because instinct tells him that he may have to run away or fight for his survival. Therefore, if a dog feels threatened or anxious, he will not lie down. Consequently, it is important to have the dog calm and relaxed as he learns the down exercise. Be encouraging and give lots of praise.

to stop traffic at an intersection. Hold the food treat in your right hand as before, but this time the food is not touching the dog's nose. He will watch the food hand and quickly learn that he is going to get that treat as soon as you return to his side.

When you can stand 1 yard away from your dog for 30 seconds, you can then begin

CONSISTENCY PAYS OFF

Dogs need consistency in their feeding schedule, exercise and toilet breaks, and in the verbal commands you use. If you use "Stay" on Monday and "Stay here, please" on Tuesday, you will confuse your dog. Don't demand perfect behavior during training sessions and then let him have the run of the house the rest of the day. Above all, lavish praise on your pet consistently every time he does something right. The more he feels he is pleasing you, the more willing he will be to learn.

building time and distance in both stays. Eventually, the dog can be expected to remain in the stay position for prolonged periods of time until you return to him or call him to you. Always praise lavishly when he stays.

TEACHING COME

If you make teaching "come" an exciting experience, you should never have a "student" that does not love the game or that fails to come when called. The secret, it seems, is never to teach the word "come."

At times when an owner most wants his dog to come when called, the owner is likely to be upset or anxious and he allows these feelings to come through in the tone of his voice when he calls his dog. Hearing that desperation in his owner's voice, the dog fears the results of going to him and therefore either disobeys outright or runs in the opposite direction. The secret, therefore, is to teach the dog a game and, when you want him to come to you, simply play the game. It is practically a no-fail solution!

To begin, have several members of your family take a few food treats and each go into a different room in the house. Take turns calling the dog, and each person should celebrate the dog's finding him with a treat and lots of happy praise. When a person calls the dog, he is actually inviting the dog to find him and get a treat as a reward for "winning."

A few turns of the "Where are you?" game and the dog will understand that everyone is playing the game and that each

Whether competing or in their everyday endeavors, the athleticism and agility of most Aussies are amazing!

The heel exercise serves as the basis for advanced obedience competition, demonstrated by this off-lead Aussie.

person has a big celebration awaiting his success at locating him. Once he learns to love the game, simply calling out "Where are you?" will bring him running from wherever he is when he hears that all-important question.

The come command is recognized as one of the most important things to teach a dog, but there are trainers who work with thousands of dogs and never teach the actual word "come."

"COME" . . . BACK

Never call your dog to come to you for a correction or scold him when he reaches you. That is the quickest way to turn a "Come" into "Go away fast!" Dogs think only in the present tense, and your dog will connect the scolding with coming to you, not with the misbehavior of a few moments earlier.

Yet these dogs will race to respond to a person who uses the dog's name followed by "Where are you?" For example, a woman has a 12-year-old companion dog who went blind, but who never fails to locate her owner when asked, "Where are you?"

Children, in particular, love to play this game with their dogs. Children can hide in smaller places like a shower or bathtub, behind a bed or under a table. The dog needs to work a little bit harder to find these hiding places but, when he does, he loves to celebrate with a treat and a tussle with a favorite youngster.

TEACHING HEEL

Heeling means that the dog walks beside the owner without pulling. It takes time and patience on the owner's part to succeed at teaching the dog that he (the owner) will not proceed unless the dog is walking calmly

A favorite chew toy can be incorporated into the Aussie's lesson plan.

FEAR AGGRESSION

Pups who are subjected to physical abuse during training commonly end up with behavioral problems as adults. One common result of abuse is fear aggression, in which a dog will lash out, bare his teeth, snarl and finally bite someone by whom he feels threatened. For example, your daughter may be playing with the dog one afternoon. As she attempts to tease him playfully, he bites her hand. Examine the cause of this behavior. Did your daughter ever hit the dog? Did someone who resembles your daughter hit or scream at the dog?

Fear aggression is relatively easy to correct. Have your daughter engage in only positive activities with the dog, such as feeding, petting and walking. She should not give any corrections or negative feedback. If the dog still growls or cowers away from her, allow someone else to accompany them. After approximately one week, the dog should feel that he can rely on her for many positive things, and he will also be prevented from reacting fearfully towards anyone who might resemble her.

beside him. Pulling out ahead on the leash is definitely not acceptable.

Begin by holding the leash in your left hand as the dog sits beside your left leg. Move the loop end of the leash to your right hand but keep your left hand short on the leash so it keeps the dog in close next to you.

Say "Heel" and step forward on your left foot. Keep the dog close to you and take three steps. Stop and have the dog sit next to you in what we now call the heel position. Praise verbally, but do not touch the dog. Hesitate a moment and begin again with "Heel," taking three steps and stopping, at which point the dog is told to sit again.

Your goal here is to have the dog walk those three steps without pulling on the leash. Once he will walk calmly beside you for three steps without pulling,

A well-trained Aussie, heeling happily at his mistress's side, is a true pleasure to walk anytime.

to heel. When you stop heeling, indicate to the dog that the exercise is over by verbally praising as you pet him and say "OK, good dog." The "OK" is used as a release word, meaning that the exercise is finished and the dog is free to relax.

If you are dealing with a dog who insists on pulling you around, simply "put on your brakes" and stand your ground until the dog realizes that the two of you are not going anywhere until he is beside you and moving at your pace, not his. It may take some time just standing there to convince the dog that you are the leader and you will be the one to decide on the direction and speed of your travel.

increase the number of steps you take to five. When he will walk politely beside you while you take five steps, you can increase the length of your walk to ten steps. Keep increasing the length of your stroll until the dog will walk quietly beside you without pulling as long as you want him

Each time the dog looks up at you or slows down to give a slack leash between the two of you, quietly praise him and say, "Good heel. Good dog." Eventually, the dog will begin to respond and within a few days he will be walking politely beside you without pulling on the leash. At first, the training sessions should be kept short and very positive; soon the dog will be able to walk nicely with you for increasingly longer distances. Remember also to give the dog free time and the opportunity to run and play when you have finished heel practice.

TUG OF WALK?

If you begin teaching the heel by taking long walks and letting the dog pull you along, he misinterprets this action as an acceptable form of taking a walk. When you pull back on the lead to counteract his pulling, he reads that tug as a signal to pull even harder!

HEELING WELL

Teach your dog to heel in an enclosed area. Once you think the dog will obey reliably and you want to attempt advanced obedience exercises such as off-lead heeling, test him in a fenced-in area so he cannot run away.

WEANING OFF FOOD IN TRAINING

Food is used in training new behaviors. Once the dog understands what behavior goes with a specific command, it is time to start weaning him off the food treats. At first, give a treat after each exercise. Then, start to give a treat only after every other exercise. Mix up the times when you offer a food reward and the times when you only offer praise so that the dog will never know when he is going to receive both food and praise and when he is going to receive only praise. This is called a variable ratio reward system and it proves successful because there is always the chance that the owner will produce a treat, so the dog never stops trying for that reward. No matter what, *always* give verbal praise.

OBEDIENCE CLASSES

It is a good idea to enroll in an obedience class if one is available in your area. If yours is to become a show dog, showing classes would be more appropriate. Many areas have dog clubs that offer basic obedience training as well as preparatory classes for obedience competition. There are also local dog trainers who offer similar classes.

In obedience trials, dogs can earn titles at various levels of competition. The beginning levels of competition include basic behaviors such as sit, down, heel, etc. The more advanced levels of competition include jumping, retrieving, scent discrimination and signal work. The advanced levels require a dog and owner to put a lot of time and effort into their training, and the titles that can be earned at these levels of competition are very prestigious.

Heel practice pays off in the show ring, as your Aussie shows off his effortless, smooth gait.

Scent determination is tested at advanced levels of obedience trials, as this Aussie's sniffer is put to work.

OTHER ACTIVITIES FOR LIFE

Whether a dog is trained in the structured environment of a class or alone with his owner at home, there are many activities that can bring fun and rewards to both owner and dog once they have mastered basic control.

Teaching the dog to help out around the home, in the yard or on the farm provides great satisfaction to both dog and owner. In addition, the dog's help makes life a little easier for his owner and raises his stature as a valued companion to his family. It helps give the dog a purpose by occupying his mind and providing an outlet for his energy. Working on a farm or a ranch is ideal for this most active herding dog, whose natural instincts drive him to work on a variety of livestock, from ducks and geese to sheep and water buffalo. Likewise, your Aussie can be entered in herding

OBEDIENCE SCHOOL

A beginner's class usually lasts for six to eight weeks. Dog and owner attend an hour-long lesson once a week and practice for a few minutes, several times a day, each day at home. If done properly, the whole procedure will result in a well-mannered dog and an owner who delights in living together harmoniously.

tests and trials, designed to develop and evaluate the dog's natural abilities.

Backpacking is an exciting and healthy activity that the dog can be taught without assistance from more than his owner. A rule of thumb for backpacking is that the dog should not be expected to carry more than one-sixth of his body weight in the pack. Excess weight on an Aussie's back could lead to difficulties.

If you are interested in participating in organized competition with your Aussie, there are activities other than obedience in which you and your dog can become involved. Agility is a popular sport where dogs run through an obstacle course that includes various jumps, tunnels and other exercises to test the dog's speed and coordination. The owners run beside their dogs to give commands and to guide them through the course. Although competitive, the focus is on fun—it's fun to do, fun to watch and great exercise.

It almost seems that agility trials were designed for the Australian Shepherds. Demanding physical agility and mental

With Olympian grace and ease, this Australian Shepherd is clearing the bar jump at an agility trial.

intelligence, plus a willingness to obey commands and please his owner, the trial's pace is set at the perfect Aussie speed—fast.

Jumping over obstacles, running through tunnels, climbing up and down seesaws and A-frame obstacles all ignite the desire to succeed in Aussies.

AGILE AUSSIES

Agility tests not only the Aussie's physical ability for coordination but also his ability to follow instructions and his intelligence to follow commands. That's why Aussies usually excel in agility competitions.

Balance, confidence and agility itself are needed for this Australian Shepherd to maneuver over the seesaw obstacle. The handler is not far away, coaxing her well-trained Aussie through the course.

HELPING PAWS

Your dog may not be the next Lassie, but every pet has the potential to do some tricks well. Identify his natural talents and hone them. Is your dog always happy and upbeat? Teach him to wag his tail or give you his paw on command. Real homebodies can be trained to do household chores, such as carrying dirty laundry or retrieving the morning paper.

Running in and out of the weave poles is a challenge they love and if they should make a mistake by missing one of the poles, many Aussies will elect to go back and do it again just to get it right!

In addition, being super-sensitive to his surroundings, the Aussie seems to respond favorably to crowd approval. The sound of audience applause frequently inspires the dog to even greater accomplishments. Though the average Aussie appears eager to tackle agility work, the wise owner restrains the dog from participating in overly ambitious activities until the dog is fully grown and bone development has ceased. Too much activity too soon can result in the early onset of arthritis later in the dog's life. Breeders recommend that dogs be 12 months of age before initiating agility training.

THE STUDENT'S STRESS TEST

During training sessions, you must be able to recognize signs of stress such as:

• tucking his tail between his legs
• lowering his head
• shivering or trembling
• standing completely still or running away
• panting and/or salivating
• avoiding eye contact
• flattening his ears back
• urinating submissively
• rolling over and lifting a leg
• grinning or baring teeth
• aggression when restrained

If your four-legged student displays these signs, he may just be nervous, stressed or intimidated. Stop for the day and try again tomorrow.

Agility trials are exciting for the Aussies, handlers and audience. You can hear the crowd cheer as this Australian Shepherd flies through the tire jump!

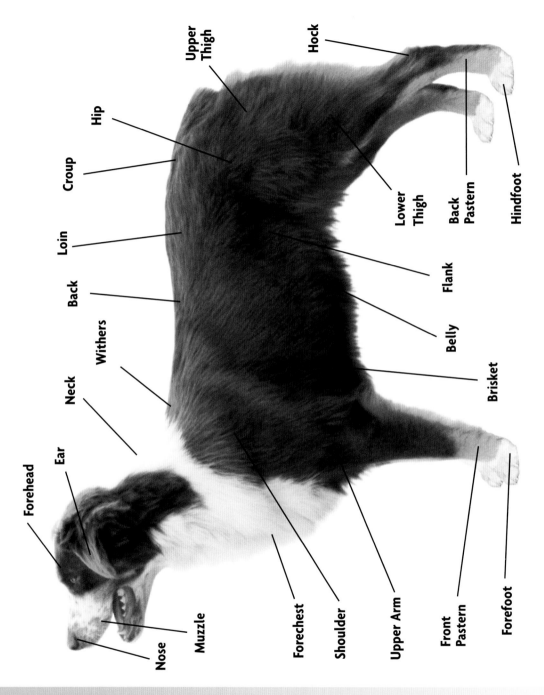

Physical Structure of the Australian Shepherd

Dogs suffer from many of the same physical illnesses as people. They might even share many of the same psychological problems. Since people usually know more about human diseases than canine maladies, many of the terms used in this chapter will be familiar but not necessarily those used by veterinarians. We will use the term *x-ray*, instead of the more acceptable term *radiograph*. We will also use the familiar term *symptoms,* even though dogs don't have symptoms, which are verbal descriptions of the patient's feelings; dogs have *clinical signs*. Since dogs can't speak, we have to look for clinical signs...but we still use the term *symptoms* in this book.

As a general rule, medicine is *practiced.* That term is not arbitrary. Medicine is a constantly changing art as we learn more and more about genetics, electronic aids (like CAT scans and MRIs) and daily laboratory advances. There are many dog maladies, like canine hip dysplasia, which are not universally treated in the same manner.

SELECTING A QUALIFIED VETERINARIAN

Your selection of a veterinarian should be based not only upon personality and ability but also upon his convenience to your home. You want a vet who is close because you might have emergencies or need to make multiple visits for treatments. You want a vet who has services that you might require such as tattooing, boarding and grooming, as well as sophisticated pet supplies and a good reputation for responsiveness. There is nothing more frustrating than having to wait a day or more to get a response from your veterinarian.

Before you buy a dog, meet and interview the veterinarians in your area. Take everything into consideration; discuss his background, specialties, fees, emergency policies, etc.

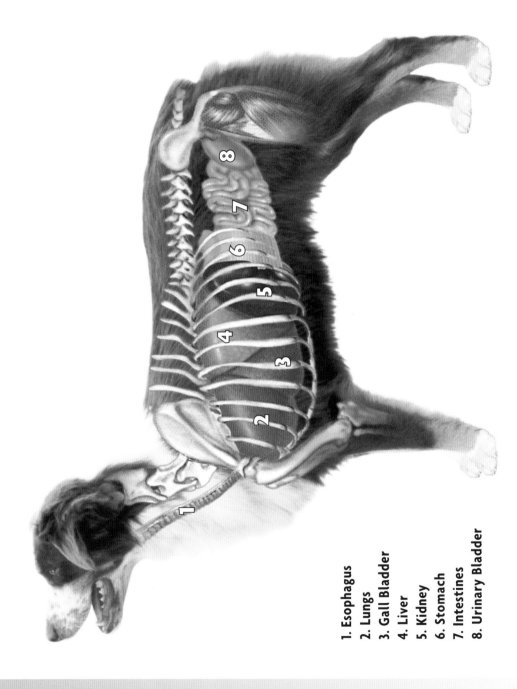

1. Esophagus
2. Lungs
3. Gall Bladder
4. Liver
5. Kidney
6. Stomach
7. Intestines
8. Urinary Bladder

Internal Organs of the Australian Shepherd

All veterinarians are licensed and their diplomas and/or certificates should be displayed in their waiting rooms. There are, however, many veterinary specialties that usually require further studies and internships. There are specialists in heart problems (veterinary cardiologists), skin problems (veterinary dermatologists), teeth and gum problems (veterinary dentists), eye problems (veterinary ophthalmologists) and x-rays (veterinary radiologists), as well as vets who have specialties in bones, muscles or certain organs. Most veterinarians do routine surgery such as neutering and stitching up wounds, as well as docking tails for breeders who require assistance. When the problem affecting your dog is serious, it is not unusual or impudent to get another medical opinion, although it is courteous to advise the vets concerned about this. You might also want to compare costs among several veterinarians. Sophisticated

Breakdown of Veterinary Income by Category

2%	Dentistry
4%	Radiology
12%	Surgery
15%	Vaccinations
19%	Laboratory
23%	Examinations
25%	Medicines

health care and veterinary services can be very costly. It is not infrequent that important decisions are based upon financial considerations.

PREVENTATIVE MEDICINE
It is much easier, less costly and more effective to practice preventative medicine than to fight bouts of illness and disease. Properly bred puppies come from parents that were selected based upon their genetic disease profiles. Their mother should have been vaccinated, free of all internal and external parasites and properly nourished. For these reasons, a visit to the veterinarian who cared for the dam is recommended. The dam can pass on disease resistance to her puppies, which can last for eight to ten weeks. She can also pass on parasites and many infections. That's why you should learn as much about the dam's health as possible.

CRYPTORCHIDISM
In adult males, when both testicles remain in the abdominal cavity, a condition known as cryptorchidism occurs. This is dangerous and can lead to serious health threats later in life. It is also a major fault and any male with one or both testicles still in the abdominal cavity may not be shown.

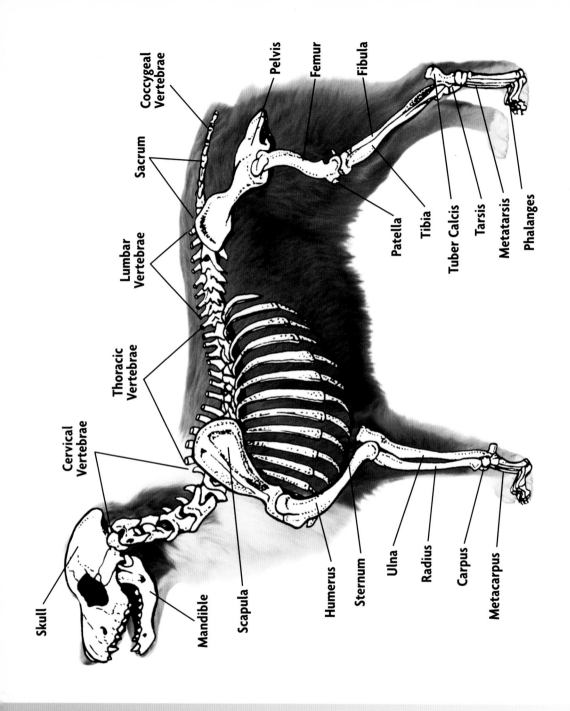

Coccygeal Vertebrae
Pelvis
Femur
Fibula
Sacrum
Patella
Tibia
Tuber Calcis
Tarsis
Metatarsis
Phalanges
Lumbar Vertebrae
Thoracic Vertebrae
Cervical Vertebrae
Skull
Mandible
Scapula
Humerus
Sternum
Ulna
Radius
Carpus
Metacarpus

Skeletal Structure of the Australian Shepherd

HEALTH AND VACCINATION SCHEDULE

Age in Weeks:	6TH	8TH	10TH	12TH	14TH	16TH	20-24TH	52ND
Worm Control	✔	✔	✔	✔	✔	✔	✔	
Neutering								✔
Heartworm		✔		✔		✔	✔	
Parvovirus	✔		✔		✔		✔	✔
Distemper		✔		✔		✔		✔
Hepatitis		✔		✔		✔		✔
Leptospirosis								✔
Parainfluenza	✔		✔		✔			✔
Dental Examination		✔					✔	✔
Complete Physical		✔					✔	✔
Coronavirus				✔			✔	✔
Kennel Cough	✔							
Hip Dysplasia								✔
Rabies							✔	

Vaccinations are not instantly effective. It takes about two weeks for the dog's immune system to develop antibodies. Most vaccinations require annual booster shots. Your veterinarian should guide you in this regard.

VACCINATION SCHEDULING

Most vaccinations are given by injection and should only be done by a veterinarian. Both he and you should keep a record of the date of the injection, the identification of the vaccine and the amount given. Some vets give a first vaccination at eight weeks, but most dog breeders prefer the course not to commence until about ten weeks because of the risk of negating any antibodies passed on by the dam. The vaccination scheduling is usually based on a 15-day cycle. You must take your vet's advice regarding when to vaccinate as this may differ according to the vaccine used. Most vaccinations immunize your puppy against viruses.

The usual vaccines contain immunizing doses of several different viruses such as distemper, parvovirus, parainfluenza and hepatitis. There are other vaccines available when the puppy is at risk. You should rely upon professional advice. This is especially true for the booster-shot program. Most vaccination programs require a booster when the puppy is a year old and once

REDUCING THE RISK
Reducing the risk of testicular cancer in males can be accomplished by neutering them as soon as possible in life. Spaying females at an early age prevents uterine cancer and reduces the risk of breast cancer.

a year thereafter. In some cases, circumstances may require more or less frequent immunizations. Kennel cough, more formally known as tracheobronchitis, is treated with a vaccine that is sprayed into the dog's nostrils. Kennel cough is usually included in routine vaccination, but this is often not as effective as the vaccines for other major diseases.

WEANING TO FIVE MONTHS OLD
Puppies should be weaned by the time they are about two months old. A puppy that remains for at least eight weeks with its mother and littermates usually adapts better to other dogs and people later in its life.

Some new owners have their puppy examined by a veterinarian immediately, which is a good idea. Vaccination programs usually begin when the puppy is very young.

The puppy will have its teeth examined and have its skeletal conformation and general health checked prior to certification by the veterinarian. Puppies in certain breeds have problems with their kneecaps, cataracts and other eye problems, heart murmurs and undescended testicles. They may also have personality problems and your veterinarian might have training in temperament evaluation.

FIVE TO TWELVE MONTHS OF AGE
Unless you intend to breed or show your dog, neutering the puppy at six months of age is recommended. Discuss this with your veterinarian. Neutering/spaying has proven to be extremely beneficial to both male and female puppies. Besides eliminating the possibility of pregnancy, it inhibits (but does not prevent) breast cancer in bitches and prostate cancer in male dogs. Under no circumstances should a bitch be spayed prior to her first season.

Your veterinarian should provide your puppy with a thorough dental evaluation at six months of age, ascertaining whether all the permanent teeth have erupted properly. A home dental-care regimen should be initiated at six months, including brushing weekly and providing good dental devices (such as nylon bones). Regular dental care promotes healthy teeth, fresh breath and a longer life.

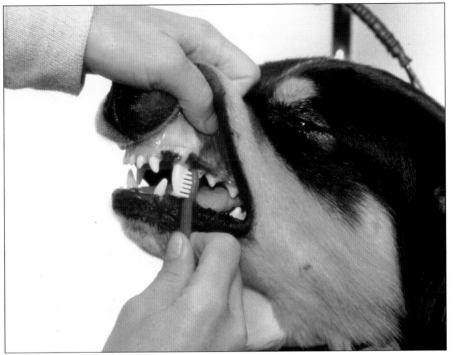

Your Aussie's teeth should be brushed regularly according to your vet's advice. You can purchase canine toothpaste and toothbrushes made especially for the task.

OVER ONE YEAR OF AGE

Once a year, your grown dog should visit the vet for an examination and vaccination boosters. Some vets recommend blood tests, thyroid-level check and dental evaluation to accompany these annual visits. A thorough clinical evaluation by the vet can provide critical background information for your dog. Blood tests are often performed at one year of age, and dental examinations around the third or fourth birthday. In the long run, quality preventative care for your pet can save money, teeth and lives.

SKIN PROBLEMS IN AUSSIES

Veterinarians are consulted by dog owners for skin problems more than for any other group of diseases or maladies. Dogs' skin is almost as sensitive as human skin and both suffer almost the same ailments (though the occurrence of acne in dogs is rare!). For this reason, veterinary dermatology has developed into a specialty practiced by many veterinarians.

Since many skin problems have visual symptoms that are almost identical, it requires the skill of an experienced veterinary dermatologist to identify and cure many of the more severe skin disorders. Pet shops sell many treatments for skin problems, but most of the treatments are directed at symptoms and not the underlying problem(s). If your dog is suffering from a skin disorder, you should seek professional assistance as quickly as possible. As with all diseases, the earlier a problem is identified and treated, the more likely is the cure.

HEREDITARY SKIN DISORDERS

Veterinary dermatologists are currently researching a number of skin disorders that are believed to have a hereditary basis. These inherited diseases are transmitted by both parents, who appear (phenotypically) normal but have a recessive gene for the disease, meaning that they carry, but are not affected by, the disease. These diseases pose serious problems to breeders because in some instances there are no methods of identifying carriers. Often the secondary diseases associated with these skin conditions are

DISEASE REFERENCE CHART

	What is it?	What causes it?	Symptoms
Leptospirosis	Severe disease that affects the internal organs; can be spread to people.	A bacterium, which is often carried by rodents, that enters through mucus membranes and spreads quickly throughout the body.	Range from fever, vomiting and loss of appetite in less severe cases to shock, irreversible kidney damage and possibly death in most severe cases.
Rabies	Potentially deadly virus that infects warm-blooded mammals.	Bite from a carrier of the virus, mainly wild animals.	1st stage: dog exhibits change in behavior, fear. 2nd stage: dog's behavior becomes more aggressive. 3rd stage: loss of coordination, trouble with bodily functions.
Parvovirus	Highly contagious virus, potentially deadly.	Ingestion of the virus, which is usually spread through the feces of infected dogs.	Most common: severe diarrhea. Also vomiting, fatigue, lack of appetite.
Kennel cough	Contagious respiratory infection.	Combination of types of bacteria and virus. Most common: *Bordetella bronchiseptica* bacteria and parainfluenza virus.	Chronic cough.
Distemper	Disease primarily affecting respiratory and nervous system.	Virus that is related to the human measles virus.	Mild symptoms such as fever, lack of appetite and mucus secretion progress to evidence of brain damage, "hard pad."
Hepatitis	Virus primarily affecting the liver.	Canine adenovirus type I (CAV-1). Enters system when dog breathes in particles.	Lesser symptoms include listlessness, diarrhea, vomiting. More severe symptoms include "blue-eye" (clumps of virus in eye).
Coronavirus	Virus resulting in digestive problems.	Virus is spread through infected dog's feces.	Stomach upset evidenced by lack of appetite, vomiting, diarrhea.

even more debilitating than the disorder itself, including cancers and respiratory problems.

Among the hereditary skin disorders, for which the mode of inheritance is known, are acrodermatitis, cutaneous asthenia (Ehlers-Danlos syndrome), sebaceous adenitis, cyclic hematopoiesis, dermatomyositis, IgA deficiency, color dilution alopecia and nodular dermatofibrosis. Some of these disorders are limited to one or two breeds and others affect a large number of breeds. All inherited diseases must be diagnosed and treated by a veterinary specialist.

PARASITE BITES

Many of us are allergic to insect bites. The bites itch, erupt and may even become infected. Dogs have the same reaction to fleas, ticks and/or mites. When an insect lands on you, you have the chance to whisk it away with your hand. Unfortunately, when your dog is bitten by a flea, tick or mite, it can only scratch it away or bite it. By the time the dog has been bitten, the parasite has done some of its damage. It may also have laid eggs to cause further problems in the near future. The itching from parasite bites is probably due to the saliva injected into the site when the parasite sucks the dog's blood.

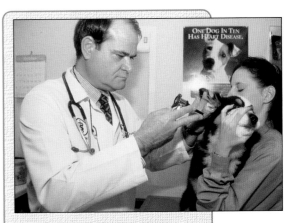

MANY KINDS OF EARS

Not every dog's ears are the same. Ears that are open to the air are healthier than ears with poor air circulation. Sometimes a dog can have two differently shaped ears. You should not probe inside your dog's ears. Only clean that which is accessible, using a cotton ball.

AUTO-IMMUNE SKIN CONDITIONS

Auto-immune skin conditions are commonly referred to as being allergic to yourself, while allergies are usually inflammatory reactions to an outside stimulus. Auto-immune diseases cause serious damage to the tissues that are involved.

The best known auto-immune disease is lupus, which affects people as well as dogs. The symptoms are variable and may affect the kidneys, bones, blood chemistry and skin. It can be fatal to both dogs and humans, though it is not thought

Acral lick syndrome is a puzzling affliction in which a dog attacks a spot, usually on its foreleg, licking it until it becomes raw.

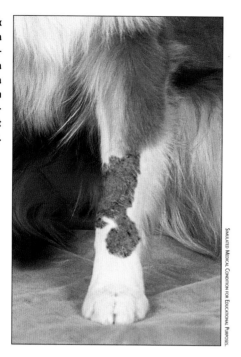

SIMULATED MEDICAL CONDITION FOR EDUCATIONAL PURPOSES.

to be transmissible. It is usually successfully treated with cortisone, prednisone or a similar corticosteroid, but extensive use of these drugs can have harmful side effects.

ACRAL LICK GRANULOMA
Many dogs have a very poorly understood syndrome called acral lick granuloma. The manifestation of the problem is the dog's tireless attack at a specific area of the body, almost always the legs or paws. The dog licks so intensively that he removes the hair and skin, leaving an ugly, large wound. Tiny protuberances, which are outgrowths

of new capillaries, bead on the surface of the wound. Owners who notice their dogs' biting and chewing at their extremities should have the vet determine the cause. If lick granuloma is identified, although there is no absolute cure, corticosteroids are the most common treatment.

AIRBORNE ALLERGIES
Just as humans have hay fever, rose fever and other fevers from which they suffer during the pollinating season, many dogs suffer from the same allergies. When the pollen count is high, your dog might suffer but don't expect him to sneeze and have a runny nose like humans. Dogs react to pollen allergies the same way they react to fleas—they scratch and bite themselves.

Dogs, like humans, can be tested for allergens. Discuss the testing with your veterinary dermatologist.

VACCINE ALLERGIES
Vaccines do not work all the time. Sometimes dogs are allergic to them and many times the antibodies, which are supposed to be stimulated by the vaccine, just are not produced. You should keep your dog in the veterinary clinic for an hour after he is vaccinated to be sure there are no allergic reactions.

FOOD PROBLEMS

FOOD ALLERGIES

Dogs are allergic to many foods that are best-sellers and highly recommended by breeders and veterinarians. Changing the brand of food that you buy may not eliminate the problem if the element to which the dog is allergic is contained in the new brand.

Recognizing a food allergy is difficult. Humans vomit or have rashes when they eat a food to which they are allergic. Dogs neither vomit nor (usually) develop rashes. They react in the same manner as they do to an airborne or flea allergy; they itch, scratch and bite, thus making the diagnosis extremely difficult. While pollen allergies and parasite bites are usually seasonal, food allergies are year-round problems.

FOOD INTOLERANCE

Food intolerance is the inability of the dog to completely digest certain foods. For example, puppies that may have done very well on their mother's milk may not do well on cow's milk. The result of this food intolerance may be loose bowels, passing gas and stomach pains. These are the only obvious symptoms of food intolerance and that makes diagnosis difficult.

TREATING FOOD PROBLEMS

It is possible to handle food allergies and food intolerance yourself. Put your dog on a diet that it has never had. Start with a single ingredient that is not in the dog's diet at the present time. Ingredients like beef or chicken are common in dogs' diets, so try something more exotic like rabbit, pheasant or another protein source. Keep the dog on this diet (with no additives) for a month. If the symptoms of food allergy or intolerance disappear, chances are your dog has a food allergy.

Don't think that the single ingredient cured the problem. You still must find a suitable diet and ascertain which ingredient in the old diet was objectionable. This is most easily done by adding ingredients to the new diet one at a time. Let the dog stay on the modified diet for a month before you add another ingredient. Eventually, you will determine the ingredient that caused the adverse reaction.

An alternative method is to carefully study the ingredients in the diet to which your dog is allergic or intolerant. Identify the main ingredient in this diet and eliminate the main ingredient by buying a different food that does not have that ingredient. Keep experimenting until the symptoms disappear after one month on the new diet.

A male dog flea, *Ctenocephalides canis.*

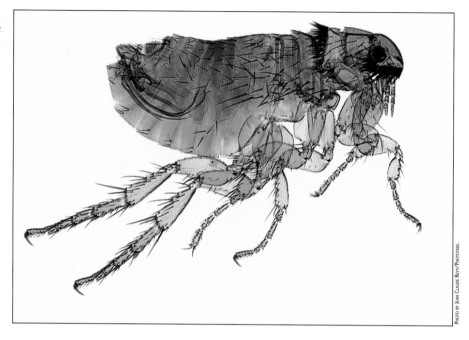

Photo by Jean Claude Revy/Phototake.

EXTERNAL PARASITES

FLEAS

Of all the problems to which dogs are prone, none is more well known and frustrating than fleas. Flea infestation is relatively simple to cure but difficult to prevent. Parasites that are harbored inside the body are a bit more difficult to eradicate but they are easier to control.

To control flea infestation, you have to understand the flea's life cycle. Fleas are often thought of as a summertime problem, but centrally heated homes have changed the patterns and fleas can be found at any time of the year. The most effective method of flea control is a two-stage approach: one stage to kill the adult fleas, and the other to control the development of pre-adult fleas. Unfortunately, no single active ingredient is effective against all stages of the life cycle.

> ### FLEA KILLER CAUTION— "POISON"
>
> Flea-killers are poisonous. You should not spray these toxic chemicals on areas of a dog's body that he licks, including his genitals and his face. Flea killers taken internally are a better answer, but check with your vet in case internal therapy is not advised for your dog.

LIFE CYCLE STAGES

During its life, a flea will pass through four life stages: egg, larva, pupa or nymph and adult. The adult stage is the most visible and irritating stage of the flea life cycle, and this is why the majority of flea-control products concentrate on this stage. The fact is that adult fleas account for only 1% of the total flea population, and the other 99% exist in pre-adult stages, i.e., eggs, larvae and nymphs. The pre-adult stages are barely visible to the naked eye.

THE LIFE CYCLE OF THE FLEA

Eggs are laid on the dog, usually in quantities of about 20 or 30, several times a day. The adult female flea must have a blood meal before each egg-laying session. When first laid, the eggs will cling to the dog's hair, as the eggs are still moist. However, they will quickly dry out and fall from the dog, especially if the dog moves around or scratches. Many eggs will fall off in the dog's favorite area or an area in which he spends a lot of time, such as his bed.

Once the eggs fall from the dog onto the carpet or furniture, they will hatch into larvae. This takes from one to ten days. Larvae are not particularly mobile and will usually travel only a few inches from where they hatch. However, they do have a tendency to move away from bright light and heavy

EN GARDE:
CATCHING FLEAS OFF GUARD!
Consider the following ways to arm yourself against fleas:
- Add a small amount of pennyroyal or eucalyptus oil to your dog's bath. These natural remedies repel fleas.
- Supplement your dog's food with fresh garlic (minced or grated) and an hearty amount of brewer's yeast, both of which ward off fleas.
- Use a flea comb on your dog daily. Submerge fleas in a cup of bleach to kill them quickly.
- Confine the dog to only a few rooms to limit the spread of fleas in the home.
- Vacuum daily...and get all of the crevices! Dispose of the bag every few days until the problem is under control.
- Wash your dog's bedding daily. Cover cushions where your dog sleeps with towels, and wash the towels often.

traffic—under furniture and behind doors are common places to find high quantities of flea larvae.

The flea larvae feed on dead organic matter, including adult flea feces, until they are ready to change into adult fleas. Fleas will usually remain as larvae for around seven days. After this period, the larvae will pupate into protective pupae. While inside the pupae, the larvae will undergo metamorphosis and change into adult fleas. This can take as little time as a few days, but the adult fleas can remain inside the pupae waiting to hatch for up to two years. The pupae are signaled to hatch by certain stimuli, such as physical pressure—the pupae's being stepped on, heat from an animal's lying on the pupae or increased carbon-dioxide levels and vibrations—indicating that a suitable host is available.

Once hatched, the adult flea must feed within a few days. Once the adult flea finds a host, it will not leave voluntarily. It only becomes dislodged by grooming or the host animal's scratching.

The adult flea will remain on the host for the duration of its life unless forcibly removed.

TREATING THE ENVIRONMENT AND THE DOG

Treating fleas should be a two-pronged attack. First, the environment needs to be treated; this includes carpets and furniture, especially the dog's bedding and areas underneath furniture. The environment should be treated with a household spray containing an Insect Growth Regulator (IGR) and an insecticide to kill the adult fleas. Most IGRs are effective against eggs and larvae; they actually mimic the fleas' own hormones and stop the eggs and larvae from developing into adult fleas. There are currently no treatments available to attack the pupa stage of the life cycle, so the adult insecticide is used to kill the newly hatched adult fleas before they find a host. Most IGRs are active for many months, while

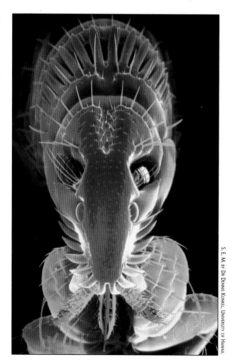

A scanning electron micrograph of a dog or cat flea, *Ctenocephalides*, magnified more than 100x. This image has been colorized for effect.

THE LIFE CYCLE OF THE FLEA

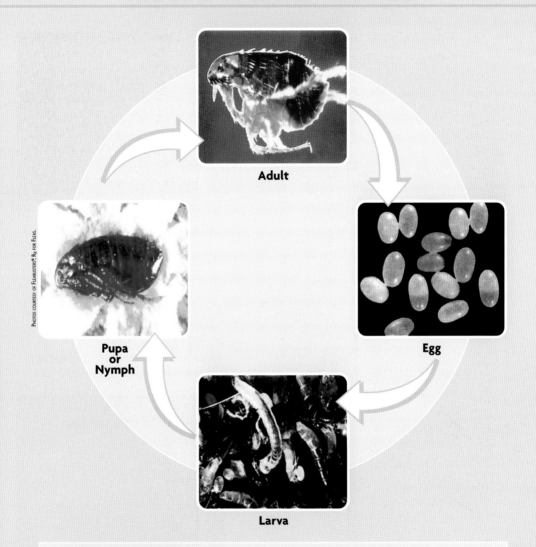

Adult

Egg

Larva

Pupa
or
Nymph

A LOOK AT FLEAS

Fleas have been around for millions of years and have adapted to changing host animals. They are able to go through a complete life cycle in less than one month or they can extend their lives to almost two years by remaining as pupae or cocoons. They do not need blood or any other food for up to 20 months.

INSECT GROWTH REGULATOR (IGR)

Two types of products should be used when treating fleas—a product to treat the pet and a product to treat the home. Adult fleas represent less than 1% of the flea population. The pre-adult fleas (eggs, larvae and pupae) represent more than 99% of the flea population and are found in the environment; it is in the case of pre-adult fleas that products containing an Insect Growth Regulator (IGR) should be used in the home.

IGRs are a new class of compounds used to prevent the development of insects. They do not kill the insect outright, but instead use the insect's biology against it to stop it from completing its growth. Products that contain methoprene are the world's first and leading IGRs. Used to control fleas and other insects, this type of IGR will stop flea larvae from developing and protect the house for up to seven months.

The American dog tick, *Dermacentor variabilis*, is probably the most common tick found on dogs. Look at the strength in its eight legs! No wonder it's hard to detach them.

adult insecticides are only active for a few days.

When treating with a household spray, it is a good idea to vacuum before applying the product. This stimulates as many pupae as possible to hatch into adult fleas. The vacuum cleaner should also be treated with an insecticide to prevent the eggs and larvae that have been collected in the vacuum bag from hatching.

The second stage of treatment is to apply an adult insecticide to the dog. Traditionally, this would be in the form of a collar or a spray, but more recent innovations include digestible insecticides that poison the fleas when they ingest the dog's blood. Alternatively, there are drops that, when placed on the back of the dog's neck, spread throughout the hair and skin to kill adult fleas.

TICKS

Though not as common as fleas, ticks are found all over the tropical and temperate world. They don't bite, like fleas; they harpoon. They dig their sharp proboscis (nose) into the dog's skin and drink the blood. Their

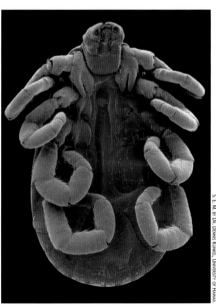

S. E. M. BY DR. DENNIS KUNKEL, UNIVERSITY OF HAWAII

only food and drink is dog's blood. Dogs can get Lyme disease, Rocky Mountain spotted fever, tick bite paralysis and many other diseases from ticks. They may live where fleas are found and they like to hide in cracks or seams in walls. They are controlled the same way fleas are controlled.

The American dog tick, *Dermacentor variabilis*, may well be the most common dog tick in many geographical areas, especially those areas where the climate is hot and humid. Most dog ticks have life expectancies of a week to six months, depending upon climatic conditions. They can neither jump nor fly, but they can crawl slowly and can range up to 6 feet to reach a sleeping or unsuspecting dog.

MITES
Just as fleas and ticks can be problematic for your dog, mites can also lead to an itchy nuisance. Microscopic in size, mites are related to ticks and generally take up permanent residence on their host animal—in this case, your dog! The term *mange* refers to any infestation caused by one of the mighty mites, of which there are six varieties that concern dog owners.

Demodex mites cause a condition known as demodicosis

DEER-TICK CROSSING
The great outdoors may be fun for your dog, but it also is a home to dangerous ticks. Deer ticks carry a bacterium known as *Borrelia burgdorferi* and are most active in the autumn and spring. When infections are caught early, penicillin and tetracycline are effective antibiotics, but if left untreated the bacteria may cause neurological, kidney and cardiac problems as well as long-term trouble with walking and painful joints.

S. E. M. BY DR. ANDREW SPIELMAN/PHOTOTAKE.

PHOTO BY DR. DENNIS KUNKEL, UNIVERSITY OF HAWAII.

The head of an American dog tick, *Dermacentor variabilis*, enlarged and colorized for effect.

The mange mite, *Psoroptes bovis*, can infest cattle and other domestic animals.

PHOTO BY JAMES HAYDEN/YOAV/PHOTOTAKE

Human lice look like dog lice; the two are closely related.

PHOTO BY DWIGHT R. KUHN.

(sometimes called red mange or follicular mange), in which the mites live in the dog's hair follicles and sebaceous glands. This type of mange is commonly passed from the dam to her puppies and usually shows up on the puppies' muzzles, though demodicosis is not transferable from one normal dog to another. Most dogs recover from this type of mange without any treatment, though topical therapies are commonly prescribed by the vet.

The *Cheyletiellosis* mite is the hook-mouthed culprit associated with "walking dandruff," a condition that affects dogs as well as cats and rabbits. This mite lives on the surface of the animal's skin and is readily transferable through direct or indirect contact with an affected animal. The dandruff is present in the form of scaly skin, which may or may not be itchy. If not treated, this mange can affect a whole kennel of dogs and can be spread to humans as well.

The *Sarcoptes* mite causes intense itching on the dog in the form of a condition known as scabies or sarcoptic mange. The cycle of the *Sarcoptes* mite lasts about three weeks, and the mites live in the top layer of the dog's skin (epidermis), preferably in areas with little hair. Scabies is highly contagious and can be passed to humans. Sometimes an allergic reaction to the mite worsens the severe itching associated with sarcoptic mange.

Ear mites, *Otodectes cynotis,* lead to otodectic mange, which most commonly affects the outer ear canal of the dog, though other areas can be affected as well. Dogs with ear-mite infestation commonly scratch at their ears, causing further irritation, and shake their heads. Dark brown droppings in the outer ear confirm the diagnosis. Your vet can prescribe a treatment to flush out the ears and kill any eggs in the ears. A complete month of treatment is necessary to cure the mange.

Two other mites, less common in dogs, include *Dermanyssus gallinae* (the poultry or red mite) and *Eutrombicula alfreddugesi* (the North American mite associated with trombiculidiasis or chigger infestation). The poultry mite frequently lives on chickens, but can transfer to dogs who spend time near farm animals. Chigger infestation affects dogs in the

NOT A DROP TO DRINK
Never allow your dog to swim in polluted water or public areas where water quality can be suspect. Even perfectly clear water can harbour parasites, many of which can cause serious to fatal illnesses in canines. Areas inhabited by water-fowl and other wildlife are especially dangerous.

Central US who have exposure to woodlands. The types of mange caused by both of these mites are treatable by veterinarians.

INTERNAL PARASITES

Most animals—fishes, birds and mammals, including dogs and humans—have worms and other parasites that live inside their bodies. According to Dr. Herbert R. Axelrod, the fish pathologist, there are two kinds of parasites: dumb and smart. The smart parasites live in peaceful cooperation with their hosts (symbiosis), while the dumb parasites kill their hosts. Most worm infections are relatively easy to control. If they are not controlled, they weaken the host dog to the point that other medical problems occur, but they do not kill the host as dumb parasites would.

A brown dog tick, *Rhipicephalus sanguineus,* is an uncommon but annoying tick found on dogs.
PHOTO BY CAROLINA BIOLOGICAL SUPPLY/PHOTOTAKE.

DO NOT MIX
Never mix pest control products without first consulting your vet. Some products can become toxic when combined with others and can cause fatal consequences.

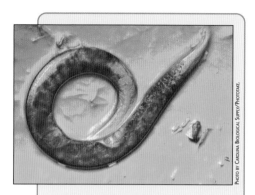

The roundworm *Rhabditis* can infect both dogs and humans.

ROUNDWORMS

Average-size dogs can pass 1,360,000 roundworm eggs every day. For example, if there were only 1 million dogs in the world, the world would be saturated with thousands of tons of dog feces. These feces would contain around 15,000,000,000 roundworm eggs.

Up to 31% of home yards and children's sand boxes in the US contain roundworm eggs.

Flushing dog's feces down the toilet is not a safe practice because the usual sewage treatments do not destroy roundworm eggs.

Infected puppies start shedding roundworm eggs at three weeks of age. They can be infected by their mother's milk.

The roundworm, *Ascaris lumbricoides.*

ROUNDWORMS

The roundworms that infect dogs are known scientifically as *Toxocara canis.* They live in the dog's intestines and shed eggs continually. It has been estimated that a dog produces about 6 or more ounces of feces every day. Each ounce of feces averages hundreds of thousands of roundworm eggs. There are no known areas in which dogs roam that do not contain roundworm eggs. The greatest danger of roundworms is that they infect people, too! It is wise to have your dog tested regularly for roundworms.

In young puppies, roundworms cause bloated bellies, diarrhea, coughing and vomiting, and are transmitted from the dam (through blood or milk). Affected puppies will not appear as animated as normal puppies. The worms appear spaghetti-like, measuring as long as 6 inches. Adult dogs can acquire roundworms through coprophagia (eating contaminated feces) or by killing rodents that carry roundworms.

Roundworm infection can kill puppies and cause severe problems in adults, as the hatched larvae travel to the lungs and trachea through the bloodstream. Cleanliness is the best preventative for roundworms. Always pick up after your dog and dispose of feces in appropriate receptacles.

PHOTO BY DWIGHT R. KUHN.

HOOKWORMS

In the United States, dog owners have to be concerned about four different species of hookworm, the most common and most serious of which is *Ancylostoma caninum,* which prefers warm climates. The others are *Ancylostoma braziliense, Ancylostoma tubaeforme* and *Uncinaria stenocephala,* the latter of which is a concern to dogs living in the Northern US and Canada, as this species prefers cold climates. Hookworms are dangerous to humans as well as to dogs and cats, and can be the cause of severe anemia due to iron deficiency. The worm uses its teeth to attach itself to the dog's intestines and changes the site of its attachment about six times per day. Each time the worm repositions itself, the dog loses

blood and can become anemic. *Ancylostoma caninum* is the most likely of the four species to cause anemia in the dog.

Symptoms of hookworm infection include dark stools, weight loss, general weakness, pale coloration and anemia, as well as possible skin problems. Fortunately, hookworms are easily purged from the affected dog with a number of medications that have proven effective. Discuss these with your veterinarian. Most heartworm preventatives include a hookworm insecticide as well.

Owners also must be aware that hookworms can infect humans, who can acquire the larvae through exposure to contaminated feces. Since the worms cannot complete their life cycle on a human, the worms simply infest the skin and cause irritation. This condition is known as cutaneous larva migrans syndrome. As a preventative, use disposable gloves or a "poop-scoop" to pick up your dog's droppings and prevent your dog (or neighborhood cats) from defecating in children's play areas.

The hookworm *Ancylostoma caninum.*

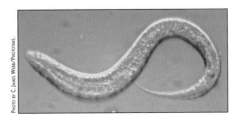

PHOTO BY C. JAMES WEBB/PHOTOTAKE.

The infective stage of the hookworm larva.

TAPEWORMS

Humans, rats, squirrels, foxes, coyotes, wolves and domestic dogs are all susceptible to tapeworm infection. Except in humans, tapeworms are usually not a fatal infection. Infected individuals can harbor 1000 parasitic worms.

Tapeworms, like some other types of worm, are hermaphroditic, meaning male and female in the same worm.

If dogs eat infected rats or mice, or anything else injected with tapeworm, they get the tapeworm disease. One month after attaching to a dog's intestine, the worm starts shedding eggs. These eggs are infective immediately. Infective eggs can live for a few months without a host animal.

The head and rostellum (the round prominence on the scolex) of a tapeworm, which infects dogs and humans.

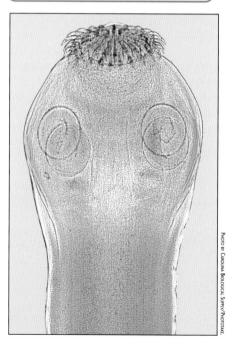

PHOTO BY CAROLINA BIOLOGICAL SUPPLY/PHOTOTAKE.

TAPEWORMS

There are many species of tapeworm, all of which are carried by fleas! The most common tapeworm affecting dogs is known as *Dipylidium caninum*. The dog eats the flea and starts the tapeworm cycle. Humans can also be infected with tapeworms—so don't eat fleas! Fleas are so small that your dog could pass them onto your hands, your plate or your food and thus make it possible for you to ingest a flea that is carrying tapeworm eggs.

While tapeworm infection is not life-threatening in dogs (smart parasite!), it can be the cause of a very serious liver disease for humans. About 50% of the humans infected with *Echinococcus multilocularis*, a type of tapeworm that causes alveolar hydatid, perish.

WHIPWORMS

In North America, whipworms are counted among the most common parasitic worms in dogs. The whipworm's scientific name is *Trichuris vulpis*. These worms attach themselves in the lower parts of the intestine, where they feed. Affected dogs may only experience upset tummies, colic and diarrhea. These worms, however, can live for months or years in the dog, beginning their larval stage in the small intestine, spending their adult stage in the large intestine and finally passing infective eggs through the dog's feces. The only way to detect whipworms is through a fecal examination, though this is not always foolproof. Treatment for whipworms is tricky, due to the worms' unusual life-cycle pattern, and very often dogs are reinfected due to exposure to infective eggs on the ground. The whipworm eggs can survive in the environment for as long as five years, thus cleaning up droppings in your own backyard as well as in public places is absolutely essential for sanitation purposes and the health of your dog.

THREADWORMS
Though less common than round-worms, hookworms and those listed above, threadworms concern dog owners in the Southwestern US and Gulf Coast area where the climate is hot and humid. Living in the small intestine of the dog, this worm measures a mere 2 millimeters and is round in shape. Like that of the whipworm, the threadworm's life cycle is very complex and the eggs and larvae are passed through the feces. A deadly disease in humans, *Strongyloides* readily infects people, and the handling of feces is the most common means of transmission. Threadworms are most often seen in young puppies; bloody diarrhea and pneumonia are symptoms. Sick puppies must be isolated and treated immediately; vets recommend a follow-up treatment one month later.

HEARTWORM PREVENTATIVES

There are many heartworm preventatives on the market, many of which are sold at your veterinarian's office. These products can be given daily or monthly, depending on the manufacturer's instructions. All of these preventatives contain chemical insecticides directed at killing heartworms, which leads to some controversy among dog owners. In effect, heartworm preventatives are necessary evils, though you should determine how necessary based on your pet's lifestyle. There is no doubt that heartworm is a dreadful disease that threatens the life of dogs. However, the likelihood of your dog's being bitten by an infected mosquito is slim in most places, and a mosquito-repellent (or an herbal remedy such as Wormwood or Black Walnut) is much safer for your dog and will not compromise his immune system (the way heartworm preventatives will). Should you decide to use the traditional preventative "medications," you can consider giving the pill every other or third month. Since the toxins in the pill will kill the heartworms at all stages of development, the pill would be effective in killing larvae, nymphs or adults and it takes four months for the larvae to reach the adult stage. Thus, there is no rationale to poisoning the dog's system on a monthly basis. Lastly, do not give the pill during the winter months since there are no mosquitoes around to pass on their infection, unless you live in a tropical environment.

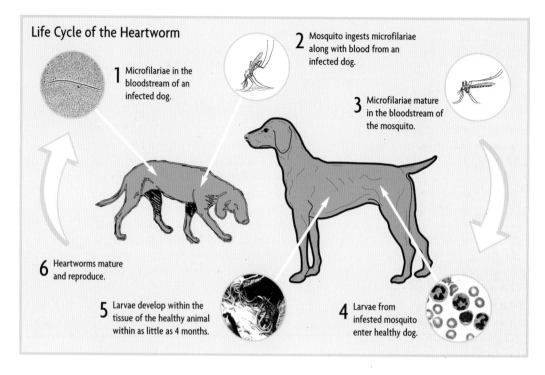

Life Cycle of the Heartworm

1 Microfilariae in the bloodstream of an infected dog.

2 Mosquito ingests microfilariae along with blood from an infected dog.

3 Microfilariae mature in the bloodstream of the mosquito.

4 Larvae from infested mosquito enter healthy dog.

5 Larvae develop within the tissue of the healthy animal within as little as 4 months.

6 Heartworms mature and reproduce.

HEARTWORMS

Heartworms are thin, extended worms up to 12 inches long, which live in a dog's heart and the major blood vessels surrounding it. Dogs may have up to 200 worms. Symptoms may be loss of energy, loss of appetite, coughing, the development of a pot belly and anemia.

Heartworms are transmitted by mosquitoes. The mosquito drinks the blood of an infected dog and takes in larvae with the blood. The larvae, called microfilariae, develop within the body of the mosquito and are passed on to the next dog bitten after the larvae mature. It takes two to three weeks for the larvae to develop to the infective stage within the body of the mosquito. Dogs are usually treated at about six weeks of age and maintained on a prophylactic dose given monthly.

Blood testing for heartworms is not necessarily indicative of how seriously your dog is infected. Although this is a dangerous disease, it is not easy for a dog to be infected. Discuss the various preventatives with your vet, as there are many different types now available. Together you can decide on a safe course of prevention for your dog.

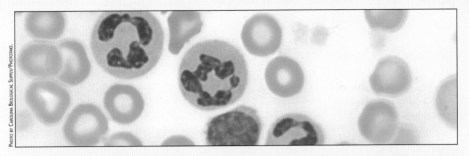

Magnified heartworm larvae, *Dirofilaria immitis*.

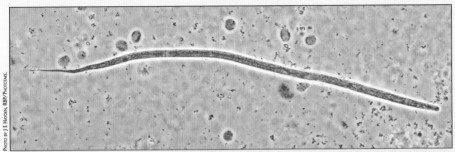

Heartworm, *Dirofilaria immitis*.

The heart of a dog infected with canine heartworm, *Dirofilaria immitis*.

HOMEOPATHY:
an alternative to conventional medicine

"Less is Most"

Using this principle, the strength of a homeopathic remedy is measured by the number of serial dilutions that were undertaken to create it. The greater the number of serial dilutions, the greater the strength of the homeopathic remedy. The potency of a remedy that has been made by making a dilution of 1 part in 100 parts (or 1/100) is 1c or 1cH. If this remedy is subjected to a series of further dilutions, each one being 1/100, a more dilute and stronger remedy is produced. If the remedy is diluted in this way six times, it is called 6c or 6cH. A dilution of 6c is 1 part in 1,000,000,000,000. In general, higher potencies in more frequent doses are better for acute symptoms and lower potencies in more infrequent doses are more useful for chronic, long-standing problems.

CURING OUR DOGS NATURALLY

Holistic medicine means treating the whole animal as a unique, perfect living being. Generally, holistic treatments do not suppress the symptoms that the body naturally produces, as do most medications prescribed by conventional doctors and vets. Holistic methods seek to cure disease by regaining balance and harmony in the patient's environment. Some of these methods include use of nutritional therapy, herbs, flower essences, aromatherapy, acupuncture, massage, chiropractic and, of course, the most popular holistic approach, homeopathy.

Homeopathy is a theory or system of treating illness with small doses of substances which, if administered in larger quantities, would produce the symptoms that the patient already has. This approach is often described as "like cures like." Although modern veterinary medicine is geared toward the "quick fix," homeopathy relies on the belief that, given the time, the body is able to heal itself and return to its natural, healthy state.

Choosing a remedy to cure a problem in our dogs is the difficult part of homeopathy. Consult with your veterinarian for a professional diagnosis of your dog's symptoms. Often these symptoms require immediate conventional care. If

your vet is willing and knowledgeable, you may attempt a homeopathic remedy. Be aware that cortisone, a popular conventional remedy, prevents homeopathic remedies from working. There are hundreds of possibilities and combinations to cure many problems in dogs, from basic physical problems such as excessive shedding, fleas or other parasites, unattractive doggy odor, bad breath, upset tummy, dry, oily or dull coat, diarrhea, obesity, poor appetite, ear problems or eye discharge (including tears and dry or mucusy matter), to behavioral abnormalities such as fear of loud noises, habitual licking, excessive barking and various phobias. From alumina to zincum metallicum, the remedies span the planet and the imagination...from flowers and weeds to chemicals, insect droppings, diesel smoke and volcanic ash.

Using "Like to Treat Like"

Unlike conventional medicines that suppress symptoms, homeopathic remedies treat illnesses with small doses of substances that, if administered in larger quantities, would produce the symptoms that the patient already has. While the same homeopathic remedy can be used to treat different symptoms in different dogs, here are some interesting remedies and their uses.

Apis Mellifica
(made from honey bee venom) can be used for allergies or to reduce swelling that occurs in acutely infected kidneys.

Diesel Smoke
can be used to help control travel sickness.

Calcarea Fluorica
(made from calcium fluoride, which helps harden bone structure) can be useful in treating hard lumps in tissues.

Natrum Muriaticum
(made from common salt, sodium chloride) is useful in treating thin, thirsty dogs.

Nitricum Acidum
(made from nitric acid) is used for symptoms you would expect to see from contact with acids such as lesions, especially where the skin joins the linings of body orifices or openings such as the lips and nostrils.

Symphytum
(made from the herb Knitbone, *Symphytum officianale*) is used to encourage bones to heal.

Urtica Urens
(made from the common stinging nettle) is used in treating painful, irritating rashes.

CDS: COGNITIVE DYSFUNCTION SYNDROME
"OLD-DOG SYNDROME"

There are many ways for you to evaluate old-dog syndrome. Veterinarians have defined CDS (cognitive dysfunction syndrome) as the gradual deterioration of cognitive abilities. These are indicated by changes in the dog's behavior. When a dog changes his routine response, and maladies have been eliminated as the cause of these behavioral changes, then CDS is the usual diagnosis.

More than half the dogs over eight years old suffer from some form of CDS. The older the dog, the more chance it has of suffering from CDS. In humans, doctors often dismiss the CDS behavioral changes as part of "winding down."

There are four major signs of CDS: frequent potty accidents inside the home, sleeping much more or much less than normal, confusion and failure to respond to social stimuli.

SYMPTOMS OF CDS

FREQUENT POTTY ACCIDENTS
- *Urinates in the house.*
- *Defecates in the house.*
- *Doesn't signal that he wants to go out.*

SLEEP PATTERNS
- *Moves much more slowly.*
- *Sleeps more than normal during the day.*
- *Sleeps less during the night.*

CONFUSION
- *Goes outside and just stands there.*
- *Appears confused with a faraway look in his eyes.*
- *Hides more often.*
- *Doesn't recognize friends.*
- *Doesn't come when called.*
- *Walks around listlessly and without a destination goal.*

FAILURE TO RESPOND TO SOCIAL STIMULI
- *Comes to people less frequently, whether called or not.*
- *Doesn't tolerate petting for more than a short time.*
- *Doesn't come to the door when you return home.*

AUSTRALIAN SHEPHERD

The term *old* is a qualitative term. For dogs, as well as their masters, old is relative. Certainly we can all distinguish between a puppy Australian Shepherd and an adult Australian Shepherd—there are the obvious physical traits, such as size, appearance and facial expressions, and personality traits. Puppies and young dogs like to play with children. Children's natural exuberance is a good match for the seemingly endless energy of young dogs. They like to run, jump, chase and retrieve. When dogs grow older and cease their interaction with children, they are often thought of as being too old to play with the kids.

On the other hand, if an Aussie is only exposed to people with quieter lifestyles, its life will normally be less active and the change in its activity level as it ages will not be as noticeable.

If people live to be 100 years old, dogs live to be 20 years old. While this is a good rule of thumb, it is very inaccurate. When trying to compare dog years to human years, you cannot make a generalization about all dogs. The average lifespan of the Australian Shepherd is 11 to 15 years, with 12 being the mean age, which is quite good compared to many other pure-bred dogs that may only live to 8 or 9 years of age. Dogs are generally considered mature within three years, but they can reproduce even earlier. So the first three years of a dog's life are like seven times that of comparable humans. That means a 3-year-old dog is like a 21-year-old human. As the curve of comparison shows, there is no

COPING WITH LOSS

When your dog dies, you may be as upset as when a human companion passes away. You are losing your protector, your baby, your confidante and your best friend. Many people experience not only grief but also feelings of guilt and doubt as to whether they did all that they could for their pet. Allow yourself to grieve and mourn, and seek help from friends and support groups. You may also wish to consult books and websites that deal with this topic.

hard and fast rule for comparing dog and human ages. The comparison is made even more difficult, for not all humans age at the same rate...and human females live longer than human males.

WHAT TO LOOK FOR IN SENIORS

Most veterinarians and breeders use the eight-year mark as the time to consider an Aussie a senior. The term *senior* does not imply that the dog is geriatric and has begun to fail in mind and body. Aging is essentially a slowing process. Humans readily admit that they feel a difference in their activity level from age 20 to 30, and then from 30 to 40, etc. By treating the eight-year-old dog as a senior, owners are able to implement certain therapeutic and preventative medical strategies with the help of their veterinarians. A senior-care program should include at least two veterinary visits per year and screening sessions to determine the dog's health status, as well as nutritional counseling. Veterinarians determine the senior dog's health status through a blood smear for a complete blood count, serum chemistry profile with electrolytes, urinalysis, blood pressure check, electrocardiogram, ocular tonometry (pressure on the eyeball) and dental prophylaxis.

Such an extensive program for senior dogs is well advised before owners start to see the obvious physical signs of aging, such as slower and inhibited movement, graying, increased sleep/nap periods and disinterest in play and other activity. This preventative program promises a longer, healthier life for the aging

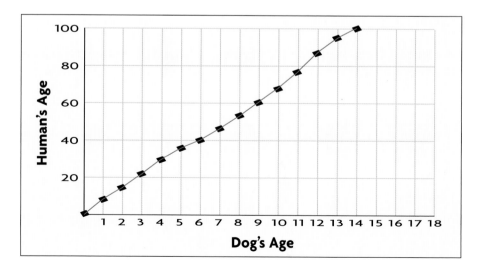

dog. Among the physical problems common in aging dogs are the loss of sight and hearing, arthritis, kidney and liver failure, diabetes mellitus, heart disease and Cushing's disease (a hormonal disease).

In addition to the physical manifestations discussed, there are some behavioral changes and problems related to aging dogs. Dogs suffering from hearing or vision loss, dental discomfort or arthritis can become aggressive. Likewise, the near-deaf and/or blind dog may be startled more easily and react in an unexpectedly aggressive manner. Seniors suffering from senility can become more impatient and irritable. Housesoiling accidents are associated with loss of mobility, kidney problems and loss of sphincter control as well as plaque accumulation, physiological brain changes and reactions to medications. Older dogs, just like young puppies, suffer from separation anxiety, which can lead to excessive barking, whining, housesoiling and destructive behavior. Seniors may become fearful of everyday sounds, such as vacuum cleaners, heaters, thunder and passing traffic. Some dogs have difficulty sleeping, due to discomfort, the need for frequent potty visits and the like.

Owners should avoid spoiling the older dog with too many fatty treats. Obesity is a common

---

NOTICING THE SYMPTOMS

The symptoms listed below are symptoms that gradually appear and become more noticeable. They are not life-threatening; however, the symptoms below are to be taken very seriously and warrant a discussion with your veterinarian:

- Your dog cries and whimpers when he moves, and he stops running completely.
- Convulsions start or become more serious and frequent. The usual convulsion (spasm) is when the dog stiffens and starts to tremble, being unable or unwilling to move. The seizure usually lasts for 5 to 30 minutes.
- Your dog drinks more water and urinates more frequently. Wetting and bowel accidents take place indoors without warning.
- Vomiting becomes more frequent.

---

problem in older dogs and subtracts years from their lives. Keep the senior dog as trim as possible since excessive weight puts additional stress on the body's vital organs. Some breeders recommend supplementing the diet with foods high in fiber and lower in calories. Adding fresh vegetables and marrow broth to the senior's diet makes a tasty, low-calorie, low-fat supplement. Vets also offer specialty diets for senior dogs that are worth exploring.

Your dog, as he nears his twilight years, needs his owner's patience and good care more than ever. Never punish an older dog for an accident or abnormal behavior. For all the years of love, protection and companionship that your dog has provided, he deserves special attention and courtesies. The older dog may need to relieve himself at 3 a.m. because he can no longer hold it for eight hours. Older dogs may not be able to remain crated for more than two or three hours. It may be time to give up a sofa or chair to your old friend. Although he may not seem as enthusiastic about your attention and petting, he does appreciate the considerations you offer as he gets older.

Your Australian Shepherd does not understand why his world is slowing down. Owners must make the transition into the golden years as pleasant and rewarding as possible.

WHAT TO DO WHEN THE TIME COMES

You are never fully prepared to make a rational decision about putting your dog to sleep. It is very obvious that you love your

Consult with your veterinarian to help find a pet cemetery in your area.

Aussie or you would not be reading this book. Putting a loved dog to sleep is extremely difficult. It is a decision that must be made with your veterinarian. You are usually forced to make the decision when one of the life-threatening symptoms described herein becomes serious enough for you to seek veterinary help.

If the prognosis of the malady indicates the end is near and your beloved pet will only suffer more and experience no enjoyment for the balance of its life, then euthanasia is the right choice.

WHAT IS EUTHANASIA?

Euthanasia derives from the Greek meaning *good death*. In other words, it means the planned, painless killing of a dog suffering from a painful, incurable condition, or who is so aged that it cannot walk, see, eat or control its excretory functions.

Euthanasia is usually accomplished by injection with an overdose of an anesthesia or barbiturate. Aside from the prick of the needle, the experience is usually painless.

WEATHERING OLD AGE

Elderly Aussies, those over eight years of age, are less able to cope with extremes in weather conditions. Owners need to take this into consideration as their Aussies age.

Cremation is an option for those who wish to memorialize their deceased pets. Pet cemeteries usually have areas to accommodate urns that contain the dogs' ashes.

MAKING THE DECISION

The decision to euthanize your dog is never easy. The days during which the dog becomes ill and the end occurs can be unusually stressful for you. If this is your first experience with the death of a loved one, you may need the comfort dictated by your religious beliefs. If you are the head of the family and have children, you should have involved them in the decision of putting your Australian Shepherd to sleep. Usually your dog can be maintained on drugs for a few days in order to give you ample time to make a decision. During this time, talking with members of your family or even people who have lived through this same experience can ease the burden of your inevitable decision.

THE FINAL RESTING PLACE

Dogs can have some of the same privileges as humans. The remains of your beloved dog can be buried in a pet cemetery, which is generally expensive. A dog who has died at home can be buried in your yard in a place suitably marked with some stone or newly planted tree or bush. Alternatively, the dog can be cremated individually and the ashes returned to you. A less expensive option is mass cremation, although, of course, the ashes cannot then be returned. Vets can usually arrange the cremation on your behalf. The cost of these options should always be discussed frankly and openly with your veterinarian.

GETTING ANOTHER DOG?

The grief of losing your beloved dog will be as lasting as the grief of losing a human friend or relative. In most cases, if your dog died of old age (if there is such a thing), it had slowed down considerably. Do you want a new Aussie puppy to replace it? Or are you better off finding a more mature Australian Shepherd, say two to three years of age, which will usually be house-trained and will have an already developed personality. In this case, you can find out if you like each other after a few hours of being together.

The decision is, of course, your own. Do you want another Australian Shepherd or perhaps a different breed so as to avoid comparison with your beloved friend? Most people usually buy the same breed because they know (and love) the characteristics of that breed. Then, too, they often know people who have the same breed and perhaps they are lucky enough that one of their friends expects a litter soon. What could be better?

AN ANCIENT ACHE

As ancient a disease as any, arthritis remains poorly explained for human and dog alike. Fossils dating back 100 million years show the deterioration caused by arthritis. Human fossils two million years old show the disease in man. The most common type of arthritis affecting dogs is known as osteoarthritis, which occurs in adult dogs before their senior years. Obesity aggravating the dog's joints has been cited as a factor in arthritis.

Rheumatoid disease destroys joint cartilage and causes arthritic joints. Pituitary dysfunctions as well as diabetes have been associated with arthritis. Veterinarians treat arthritis variously, including aspirin, "bed rest" in the dog's crate, physical therapy and exercise, heat therapy (with a heating pad), providing soft bedding materials and treatment with corticosteroids (to reduce pain and swelling temporarily). The average age of onset of arthritis in Australian Shepherds is eight years of age. Your vet will be able to recommend a course of action to help relieve your arthritic pal.

When you purchase your Australian Shepherd, you will make it clear to the breeder whether you want one just as a loveable companion and pet, or if you hope to be buying an Australian Shepherd with show prospects. No reputable breeder will sell you a young puppy and tell you that it is *definitely* of show quality, for so much can go wrong during the early months of a puppy's development. If you plan to show, what you will hopefully have acquired is a puppy with "show potential."

To the novice, exhibiting an Australian Shepherd in the show ring may look easy, but it takes a lot of hard work and devotion to do top winning at a show such as the prestigious Westminster Kennel Club dog show, not to mention a little luck too!

The first concept that the canine novice learns when watching a dog show is that each dog first competes against members of its own breed. Once the judge has selected the best member of each breed (Best of Breed), that chosen dog will compete with other dogs

in its group. Finally, the dogs chosen first in each group will compete for Best in Show.

The second concept that you must understand is that the dogs are not actually compared against one another. The judge compares each dog against its breed standard, the written description of the ideal specimen that is approved by the American Kennel Club (AKC). While some early breed standards were indeed based on specific dogs that were famous or popular, many dedicated enthusiasts say that a perfect specimen, as described in the standard, has never walked into a show ring, has never been bred and, to the woe of dog breeders around the globe, does not exist. Breeders attempt to get as close to this ideal as possible with every litter, but theoretically the "perfect" dog is so elusive that it is impossible.

If you are interested in exploring the world of dog showing, your best bet is to join your local breed club or the national parent club, which is the Australian Shepherd Club of America. These

clubs often host both regional and national specialties, shows only for Australian Shepherds, which can include conformation as well as obedience, agility and herding trials. Even if you have no intention of competing with your Aussie, a specialty is like a festival for lovers of the breed who congregate to share their favorite topic: Aussies! Clubs also send out newsletters, and some organize training days and seminars in order that people may learn more about their chosen breed. To locate the breed club closest to you, contact the American Kennel Club, which furnishes the rules and regulations for all of these events plus general dog registration and other basic requirements of dog ownership.

The American Kennel Club offers three kinds of conformation shows: an all-breed show (for all AKC-recognized breeds), a specialty show (for one breed only, usually sponsored by the parent club) and a Group show (for all breeds in the Group).

For a dog to become an AKC champion of record, the dog must accumulate 15 points at the shows from at least three different judges, including two "majors." A "major" is defined as a three-, four- or five-point win, and the number of points per win is determined on the number of dogs entered in the show on the day. Depending on the breed, the number of points that are awarded varies. In a breed as popular as the Australian Shepherd, more dogs are needed to rack up the points. At any dog show, only one dog and one bitch of each breed can win points.

Dog showing does not offer "co-ed" classes. Dogs and bitches never compete against each other in the classes. Non-champion dogs are called "class dogs" because they compete in one of five classes. Dogs are entered in a particular class depending on age and previous show wins. To begin, there is the Puppy Class (for 6- to 9-month-olds and for 9- to 12-month-olds); this class is followed by the Novice Class (for dogs that have not won any first prizes except in the Puppy Class or three first prizes in the Novice Class and have not accumulated any points toward their champion title; the Bred-by-Exhibitor Class (for dogs handled by their breeders or handled by one of the breeder's immediate family); American-bred Class (for dogs bred in the USA); and the Open Class (for any dog that is not a champion).

The judge at the show begins judging the Puppy Class, first dogs and then bitches, and proceeds through the classes. The judge places his winners first through fourth in each class. In the Winners Class, the first-place winners of each class compete with one

A line of lovely Australian Shepherds, with their handlers, await and prepare for examination by the judge at an outdoor conformation show.

another to determine Winners Dog and Winners Bitch. The judge also places a Reserve Winners Dog and Reserve Winners Bitch, which could be awarded the points in the case of a disqualification. The Winners Dog and Winners Bitch are the two that are awarded the points for the breed, then compete with any champions of record entered in the show. The judge reviews the Winners Dog, Winners Bitch and all the other champions to select his Best of Breed. The Best of Winners is selected between the Winners Dog and Winners Bitch. Were one of these two to be selected Best of Breed, it would automatically be named Best of Winners as well. Finally the judge selects his Best of Opposite Sex to the Best of Breed winner.

At a Group show or all-breed show, the Best of Breed winners from each breed then compete against one another for Group One through Group Four. The judge compares each Best of Breed to its breed standard, and the dog that most closely lives up to the ideal for its breed is selected as Group

MEET THE AKC

American Kennel Club is the main governing body of the dog sport in the United States. Founded in 1884, the AKC consists of 500 or more independent dog clubs plus 4,500 affiliate clubs, all of which follow the AKC rules and regulations. Additionally, the AKC maintains a registry for pure-bred dogs in the US and works to preserve the integrity of the sport and its continuation in the country. Over 1,000,000 dogs are registered each year, representing about 150 recognized breeds. There are over 15,000 competitive events held annually for which over 2,000,000 dogs enter to participate. Dogs compete to earn over 40 different titles, from champion to Companion Dog to Master Agility Champion.

One. Finally, all seven group winners (from the Herding Group, Toy Group, Hound Group, etc.) compete for Best in Show.

To find out about dog shows in your area, you can subscribe to the American Kennel Club's monthly magazine, the *American Kennel Gazette,* and the accompanying Events Calendar. You can also look in your local newspaper for advertisements for dog shows in your area or go on the Internet to the AKC's website, www.akc.org.

If your Australian Shepherd is six months of age or older and registered with the AKC, you can enter him in a dog show where the breed is offered classes. Provided that your Australian Shepherd does not have a disqualifying fault, he can compete. Only unaltered dogs can be entered in a dog show, so if you have spayed or neutered your Australian Shepherd, you cannot compete in conformation shows. The reason for this is simple. Dog shows are the main forum to prove which representatives in a breed are worthy of being bred. Only dogs that have achieved championships—the AKC "seal of approval" for quality in pure-bred dogs—should be bred. Altered dogs, however, can participate in other AKC events such as the various trials and the Canine Good Citizen program.

OBEDIENCE TRIALS

Obedience trials in the US trace back to the early 1930s when organized obedience training was developed to demonstrate how well dog and owner could work together. The pioneer of obedience trials is Mrs. Helen Whitehouse Walker, a Standard Poodle fancier, who designed a series of exercises after the Associated Sheep, Police Army Dog Society of Great Britain. Since the days of Mrs. Walker, obedience trials have grown by leaps and bounds, and today there are over 2,000 trials held in the US every year, with more than 100,000 dogs competing. Any registered AKC dog can enter an obedience trial, regardless of conformational disqualifications or neutering.

Obedience trials are divided into three levels of progressive difficulty. At the first level, the

---

BECOMING A CHAMPION

An official AKC champion of record requires that a dog accumulate 15 points under three different judges, including two "majors" under different judges. Points are awarded based on the number of dogs entered into competition, varying from breed to breed and place to place. A win of three, four or five points is considered a "major." The AKC annually assigns a schedule of points to adjust to the variations that accompany a breed's popularity and the population of a given area.

Australian Shepherd breed judging—the judge takes a final walk past the line of dogs as he considers his decision.

Novice, dogs compete for the title Companion Dog (CD); at the intermediate level, the Open, dogs compete for the title Companion Dog Excellent (CDX); and at the advanced level, dogs compete for the title Utility Dog (UD). Classes are sub-divided into "A" (for beginners) and "B" (for more experienced handlers). A perfect score at any level is 200, and a dog must score 170 or better to earn a "leg," of which three are needed to earn the title. To earn points, the dog must score more than 50% of the available points in each exercise; the possible points range from 20 to 40.

Each level consists of a different set of exercises. In the Novice level, the dog must heel on- and off-lead, come, long sit, long down and stand for examination. These skills are the basic ones required for a well-behaved "Companion Dog." The Open level requires that the dog perform the same exercises above but without a leash for extended lengths of time, as well as retrieve a dumbbell, broad jump and drop on recall. In the Utility level, dogs must perform ten difficult exercises, including scent discrimination, hand signals for basic commands, directed jump and directed retrieve.

Once a dog has earned the UD title, he can compete with other proven obedience dogs for the coveted title of Utility Dog Excellent (UDX), which requires that the dog win "legs" in ten shows. Utility Dogs who earn "legs" in Open B and Utility B earn points toward their Obedience Trial Champion title. In 1977 the title Obedience Trial Champion (OTCh.) was established by the AKC. To become an OTCh., a dog needed to earn 100 points, which requires three first places in Open B and Utility under three different judges.

AGILITY TRIALS

Having had its origins in the UK back in 1977, AKC agility had its official beginning in the US in August 1994, when the first licensed agility trials were held. The AKC allows all registered breeds to participate, providing the dog is 12 months of age or older. Agility is designed so that the handler demonstrates how well the dog can work at his side. The handler directs his dog over an obstacle course that includes jumps as well as tires, the dog walk, weave poles, pipe tunnels, collapsed tunnels, etc. While working his way through the course, the dog must keep one eye and ear on the handler and the rest of his body on the course. The handler gives verbal and hand signals to guide the dog through the course.

The first organization to promote agility trials in the US was the United States Dog Agility Association, Inc. (USDAA), which was established in 1986 and spawned numerous member clubs around the country. Both the USDAA and the AKC offer titles to winning dogs.

Three titles are available through the USDAA: Agility Dog (AD), Advanced Agility Dog (AAD) and Master Agility Dog (MAD). The AKC offers Novice Agility (NA), Open Agility (OA), Agility Excellent (AX) and Master Agility Excellent (MX). Beyond these four AKC titles, dogs can win additional ones in "jumper" classes, Jumpers with Weave Novice (NAJ), Open (OAJ) and Excellent (MXJ), which lead to the ultimate title(s): MACH, Master Agility Champion. Dogs can continue to add number designations to the MACH titles, indicating how many times the dog has met the MACH requirements, such as MACH1, MACH2, etc.

HERDING TESTS AND TRIALS

Since the first sheepdog trials recorded in the late 19th century in Wales, the practice of herding trials has grown tremendously around the world. The first trial began as a friendly match to see which farmer's dog was the best at moving sheep. Today the sport is more organized than in those early days, and all herding breeds can earn titles at these fun and competitive events.

A GENTLEMAN'S SPORT

Whether or not your dog wins top honors, showing is a pleasant social event. Sometimes, one may meet a troublemaker or nasty exhibitor, but these people should be ignored and forgotten. In the extremely rare case that someone threatens or harasses you or your dog, you can lodge a complaint with the hosting kennel club. This should be done with extreme prudence. Complaints are investigated seriously and should never be filed on a whim.

The AKC offers herding trials and tests to any herding dog that is nine months of age or older. The handler is expected to direct the Aussie to herd various livestock, including sheep, ducks, goats and cattle. There are two titles for herding tests, Herding Tested (HT) and Pre-Trial Tested (PT). If the dog shows a basic innate ability, it is awarded an HT title; the PT title is awarded to a dog that can herd a small herd of livestock through a basic course.

In herding trials, there are four titles awarded: Herding Started (HS), Herding Intermediate (HI), Herding Excellent (HX) and Herding Champion (HCh), the latter of which is awarded to a dog who has demonstrated mastery of herding in the most demanding of circumstances. Like shows, herding trials are judged against a set of standards as well as other dogs.

TRACKING

Any dog is capable of tracking, using its nose to follow a trail and the author is happy to report that the Aussie is a natural. Tracking tests are exciting and competitive ways to test your Aussie's ability to search and rescue. The AKC started tracking tests in 1937, when the first AKC-licensed test took place as part of the Utility level at an obedience trial. Ten years later in 1947, the AKC offered the first title, Tracking Dog

(TD). It was not until 1980 that the AKC added the Tracking Dog Excellent title (TDX), which was followed by the Versatile Surface Tracking title (VST) in 1995. The title Champion Tracker (CT) is awarded to a dog who has earned all three titles.

In the beginning level of tracking, the owner follows the dog through a field on a long leash. To earn the TD title, the dog must follow a track laid by a human 30 to 120 minutes prior. The track is about 500 yards with up to five directional changes. The TDX requires that the dog follow a track that is three to five hours old over a course up to 1,000 yards with up to seven directional changes. The VST requires that the dog follow a track up to five hours old through an urban setting.

Aussies excel at agility trials and seem to have wings as they fly over the jumps.

INDEX

My Australian Shepherd

PUT YOUR PUPPY'S FIRST PICTURE HERE

Dog's Name _____

Date _____ Photographer _____